I0804591

THE WIT & WISDOM OF

PATRICK BAUDE

THE WIT & WISDOM OF

PATRICK BAUDE

EXPLORING THE GOOD LIFE IN BLOOMINGTON

PATRICK BAUDE
EDITED BY WILLIAM BAUDE

AMERICAN PALATE

Published by American Palate
A Division of The History Press
Charleston, SC 29403
www.historypress.net

Copyright © 2012 by William Baude
All rights reserved

Front cover image of Pat Baude courtesy of Indiana University. Taken by Annalese Pcorman, 1995.

Special thanks to Bill Oliver, Kathleen Oliver, Todd Humerickhouse and Oliver Winery.
All photography by Chris Howard unless otherwise noted.

First published 2012

Manufactured in the United States

ISBN 978.1.60949.816.0

Library of Congress CIP data applied for.

Notice: The information in this book is true and complete to the best of our knowledge. It is offered without guarantee on the part of the author or The History Press. The author and The History Press disclaim all liability in connection with the use of this book.

All rights reserved. No part of this book may be reproduced or transmitted in any form whatsoever without prior written permission from the publisher except in the case of brief quotations embodied in critical articles and reviews.

Contents

FOREWORD

For nearly five years, Patrick wrote about wine for *Bloom Magazine*. There are quite a few wine columns in quite a few publications, but Patrick's column was different, because he wasn't just writing about wine, he was writing about life. He did so with insight and humor and with a common touch that made what he wrote engaging for everyone in the community—people knowledgeable about wine, people seeking wine knowledge and people with no interest in the subject at all. Like me. Yet we could all learn something from this fine, uncommon man.

My first encounter with Patrick's writing came when Christine Barbour, political scientist and food columnist, directed me to his wine blog. It was spring 2006, and I was preparing to launch *Bloom Magazine* here in Bloomington, Indiana. I remember reading one of his blog posts—and then another and another and another. His posts—essays about wine and occasionally beer—were smart, witty, warm, whimsical and full of information. They didn't talk up, and they didn't talk down. There was no pretense (a particular plague among wine columnists); they were pure Patrick.

I knew right away that I wanted him to write a wine column for the magazine. (Who could resist lines like "If Gwyneth Paltrow wants to meet me near the Spanish Steps for a glass of Brunello, I think I can clear my calendar.") But as a newcomer to Bloomington, I didn't know the extent of his following. My fear was that the whole town was reading this incredible blog and that a magazine column would be redundant. I called Patrick, introduced myself and was quickly relieved of that fear. "Only my family reads it," he assured me.

And thus began a beautiful flow of columns that ended far too soon with Patrick's passing.

Some time later, a memorial service for Patrick was planned, and I was asked to be a speaker. I was honored but apprehensive. What would I say? I had known Patrick for only five years; other speakers and most of the audience would have known him for decades.

The day of the service, the large lecture hall at the IU Maurer School of Law was packed with Patrick's family, friends, colleagues and former students. Tissue boxes were strategically located at the end of each aisle. Instead of a speech, I read vignettes from my favorite Patrick columns. It was Patrick's voice and Patrick's words; I was merely a conduit. The audience responded with waves of laughter as though Patrick was there in the room, entrancing us once again with his stories.

I hope that as you read this book, you, too, will feel his presence. And if you have the urge to laugh out loud, please do. I think Patrick would like that.

Malcolm Abrams
Editor and publisher
Bloom Magazine

Introduction

Dad spent forty years as a constitutional law professor at Indiana University, a job he clearly loved and excelled at. That's evidenced by the numerous teaching awards he won, by the glowing tributes from colleagues and former students recently published in the *Indiana Law Journal* and by the many years he spent playing with and building up ideas.

But law was not Dad's only professional passion. Dad spent close to five years as a professional wine writer for *Bloom Magazine*, especially the years right after he had retired (but was still teaching). When I described my dad to new friends during that time period, I was no longer sure whether to identify him first and foremost as a constitutional law professor or a wine writer. I almost suspected that sharing what he knew about wine had become as important to him as teaching law.

One reason for that, as you will see from his writings in this book, is that wine was not just a narrow topic for Dad. It was a frame of reference for food, for history, for cuisine—and frequently for life generally. So writing about wine was a way to write about travel, about eating, about family and about much more. (As he puts it in this book: "It must be that wine critics are not writing about wine as such…They are arguing about the good life to which wine might be a tool.")

The floor of Pat Baude's wine cellar, which held wine bottles that no longer fit on the packed shelves.

William Baude savoring a glass of wine in his dad's honor.

Writing about wine (and beer and spirits) was also a way to connect with places. Very little wine is grown in Indiana (though some is). But Dad's father was French, and it is hard to read his thoughts about French wine without sensing a familial connection. (Dad also frequently wrote about wine in California and visited wineries there—the state where I now live.)

Moreover, a major point of Dad's writings was to emphasize the local experience in finding and drinking great wines. For many years it was very hard to get expensive "boutique" wines in Indiana, where direct shipments were legally problematic and local tastes did not often support exotic preferences. But wine, for Dad, was supposed to be an unpretentious everyday pleasure, so he was eager to demonstrate that you could live well (and drink well) without living in California or New York or Paris.

There is more of a local element to beer. There are multiple good, local breweries in Bloomington (discussed in "Here's to Beer!"), and many more scattered throughout the Midwest. Perhaps the most place-inspired of all is bourbon whiskey, most of which is made just across the southern Indiana border in Kentucky. Bourbon does not feature as extensively in these writings, but Dad also grew quite fascinated with it.

The chance to write about locally available wines (and local beer and spirits)—as well as the rise of *Bloom Magazine* itself—is also connected to the growth in Bloomington's food scene. There are several Bloomington establishments that are mentioned again and again in these pages (like the inimitable Restaurant Tallent), which made Bloomington an excellent place to be a foodie. It's hard to imagine most of them existing in 1968, when Dad first arrived.

Finally, a few words on the contents of this book. Most of the wine writing in the book comes from my father's columns, published in *Bloom Magazine*, under Malcolm Abrams. They are presented in chronological order, but as you will see, most of what they contain is timeless. After that come several miscellaneous observations on wine and making spirits, some of which were once published on my father's blog. There also two short pieces with a slightly more academic flair. "Memory and the Twenty-First Amendment" is an extended abstract of a presentation for the 2007 Annual Meeting of the Association for the Study of Law, Culture and the Humanities; "The Hermeneutics of Wine Criticism" was written for a symposium at Oxford in 2009. "Memory and the Twenty-First Amendment" may be my favorite thing Dad ever wrote about the law. Finally come two tributes, both originally from *Bloom*. The accompanying pictures were taken by Chris Howard, of CM Howard Photography (Bernal Heights, San Francisco).

William Baude

To Pair or Not to Pair

(August/September 2006)

There is disagreement in matters of taste between those who demand that poems rhyme and music have familiar structure, and those who relish free verse and Thursday nights at Bear's Place. So too with wine. Purists insist wines be paired appropriately, while others say to drink what we like with food we like, period. The theory of pairing is beyond me, but it's fun to test it with a couple of the traditional wine-food matches. And now is the right time to try two of them in Bloomington, with help from the farmers' market.

For one, buy a goat cheese from Capriole Farms. I'd choose the Wabash Cannonball, but any will work. By itself, a good goat cheese is a little chalky and a little, well, goaty. What's needed is a wine with vibrant acidity, tangy fruit flavors and a clean, minerally background. Time for sauvignon blanc. There are a couple of moderately priced examples that work beautifully. The 2004 Sancerre Chavignol, made by Gérard Boulay, is a brilliant wine that smells like limes with hints of all kinds of fruit and flowers and something like the clean summery smell of pebbles in the sun. The Boulay is available at Big Red, priced in the low twenties. For a few dollars less, try a South African version, 2004 Sincerely Sauvignon Blanc by Neil Ellis, available at Big Red or Tutto Bène (where you can try a glass first), and see if you like its clean grapefruit and smooth stony feel. To get the full effect, be sure to have both cheese and wine in your mouth at the same time, not just alternating bites and sips.

Pairing goat cheese and sauvignon blanc.

Pairing mushrooms and pinot noir.

For the second pairing, buy some shitake and oyster mushrooms at the market and sauté them over noodles or whatever you like. These earthy flavors need a subtle wine, one that has some clean bright fruit to lift the dish from the forest floor but also adds its own woodsy notes—a job for pinot noir. The various 2005s from Oregon should be arriving in late summer, and as soon as I can, I plan to sauté some mushrooms and open a bottle of Cloudline pinot. Another fine pinot, from New Zealand, is Waimea's 2004 Estate Pinot Noir, at Tutto Bène. I found a scent of cranberries and plums with an appetizing touch of bitterness.

I do like free verse and improvisation. Still, there's a lot to be said for planned drinking. And there are other famously perfect matches: oysters and Chablis, porterhouse and Napa cabernet, lip gloss (any flavor) and Champagne.

Austrian Wines Offer Good Choices for Real Life

(October/November 2006)

With wine, as with many other things, celebrity fantasies can lead you astray. It's wonderful to imagine drinking famous wine with beautiful people in glamorous places. If Gwyneth Paltrow wants to meet me near the Spanish Steps for a glass of Brunello, I think I can clear my calendar. But real life can be deeper by far, meeting old friends for an interesting wine none of us has drunk before. Austrian wines are good choices for real life.

A thirsty, land-locked country, Austria has had little left for export until recently. Its isolation from the international scene has left it with individualistic wines, mostly from unfamiliar grapes, created without the standard tricks that often make wines from Sonoma, the Rhône and Tuscany seem pedestrian.

Of these Austrian wines, the easiest to find are those made from the grüner veltliner grape. One good example is Rudi Pichler's Federspiel, 2004. The wine is pale gold, with sunny highlights and a few bubbles remaining from fermentation. I was struck by its scent of limes and honey and its flavor of tart apples, grapefruit and a hint of apricot. The texture is close to creamy, surprising in a wine with such an airy profile. The fresh and juicy acidity of the wine practically forces your lips into a smile—which would happen voluntarily anyway. The Federspiel would be a fine companion to a substantial fish dish or a light meat with a little

Wine for the picnic basket.

richness—I can't stop thinking of wienerschnitzel when I drink it—but I have to admit it is also a good balance for a mountain cheese like Piave or Gruyere. If you're not hungry, Mozart works too. The Pichler is available at Big Red or Tutto Bène by the bottle (cost is in the high twenties) and, at the latter, by the glass.

There's a simpler version in the new wine section at Sahara Mart. Singing Grüner Veltliner from Lenz Moser, for $12, is a sparkly yellow wine with a shy nose, a rich texture and a citrus bite. If you could make lemonade from grapes, this is what it would be like.

In general, Grüners are food friendly, their freshness often a counterpoint to hard-to-match foods like fried chicken, so they're a great choice for the picnic basket. This particular wine is a delightful surprise with fried catfish, balancing the fat with acidity and spiking the flavor like lemon juice. The problem here is that southern Indiana's great catfish mostly comes from the kind of joint that doesn't have a sommelier who thought to lay in a few first-rate grüner veltliners.

A Family Wine Dispute—Settled!

(December 2006/January 2007)

One daughter likes funky French wine and nouvelle vague films, tastes of the earth's minerals and evocations of other places and times past. One son likes New World "fruit bombs" and Firefly, sweet scents of berries in the sun and foreshadowings of the future. Fair enough, but what to serve with the holiday roast? She would like Raquillet's Mercurey Vielles Vignes 2002, a complex Burgundy with flavors of autumn leaves, leather and licorice. He would like Teusner's 2005 Joshua, an Australian wine tasting of black cherries and spicy herbs. Both are available in the low thirties at Big Red. I could serve both. But the other son and daughter are happy with Perrier, so I would be forced to cast the deciding vote on the wine.

For wine lovers, solving such puzzles is part of the fun of family celebrations. And I have done so this year. The solution is Domaine du Dragon 2004, Cuvée St. Michel. The wine is made in Provence, halfway between the traditional vineyards of the Rhône and the innovative wineries of the Languedoc. Some of the grapes are traditional to this part of southern France, like the syrah and grenache that define, for example, Chateauneuf du Pape. But 35 percent of the mix is cabernet sauvignon, a grape so modern and surprising in Provence that its use there is—no kidding—a major theme in Peter Mayle's novel *A Good Year*, now a movie with Russell Crowe.

The Dragon is inexpensive enough ($18 at Big Red) that I can actually afford to be generous with it at a large holiday table. But there is enough complexity here to keep a wine buff contemplating his glass while others are simply having a good time. The color is a very dark red, the nose full of plum—or is it blackberry or even blueberry? Sniff some more. It's certainly not red fruit, and there's a hint of menthol. Someone has also detected a whiff of tobacco. I was disappointed that I didn't: finding menthol and tobacco together would have been the first time I smelled Salem cigarettes in a wine glass. Then there is a satiny texture and a little bite. And you can actually use your watch to time how long the taste remains after you swallow—a good thirty seconds or more. You've got complexity and originality for the artist, fruit and satin for the hedonist. This is the real deal.

What's more, at the price, I'd have enough left over to stop by Tutto Bène to share a bottle of Champagne. I like the Pol Roger Brut Réserve ($90). This is a juicy wine with scents of apple and pear and an elegant taste of slate. Or we could pick up a bottle of the Pol Roger at Big Red and go home to argue about movies—maybe *Casablanca*. Do we love Ilsa because she gave up her future or admire Rick because he throws away his past? In any case, the two share a taste for the same Champagne, a Mumm Cordon Rouge. (Major Strasser drank Veuve Clicquot.)

The Good Old, Bad Old Days

(February/March 2007)

When I came to Bloomington for a job interview in 1967, my hosts served a Bernkasteler Doktor, about which I remember nothing, and a 1964 Chateau Lafite Rothschild, which I recall only because it was so disappointing. True, you could buy Lafite for $15 a bottle back then, and I saw the Bernkasteler for $12 in a liquor store window on Third Street, gleaming seductively in the ruinous sunlight.

But in those days, wines crossed the Atlantic as ordinary cargo in uncooled crates, and the temperature was unregulated in the trucks that brought them here. The bottles cooked slowly on loading docks in summer, rested in warehouses with no air conditioning and sat around in warm retail shops, perhaps for a year, until suckers like me bought them. Often the wines were fined (a clarifying process), filtered, stabilized and "conditioned" for the hardships of travel, a process absolutely guaranteed to take the life out of them.

I use these memories to temper my nostalgia. By comparison, wine today arrives here in better shape, and it's also a fantastic bargain. Not the Lafite—the most recent vintage runs $700—but there are modest wines, carefully made, shipped by importers who are fanatical about conditions (like Kermit Lynch or Vintner Select) and held by attentive sellers (like Big Red) that will easily outclass abused celebrity wines. Of course you can

A Bernkasteler from Pat Baude's cellar—where it was kept safe from the ruinous sunlight.

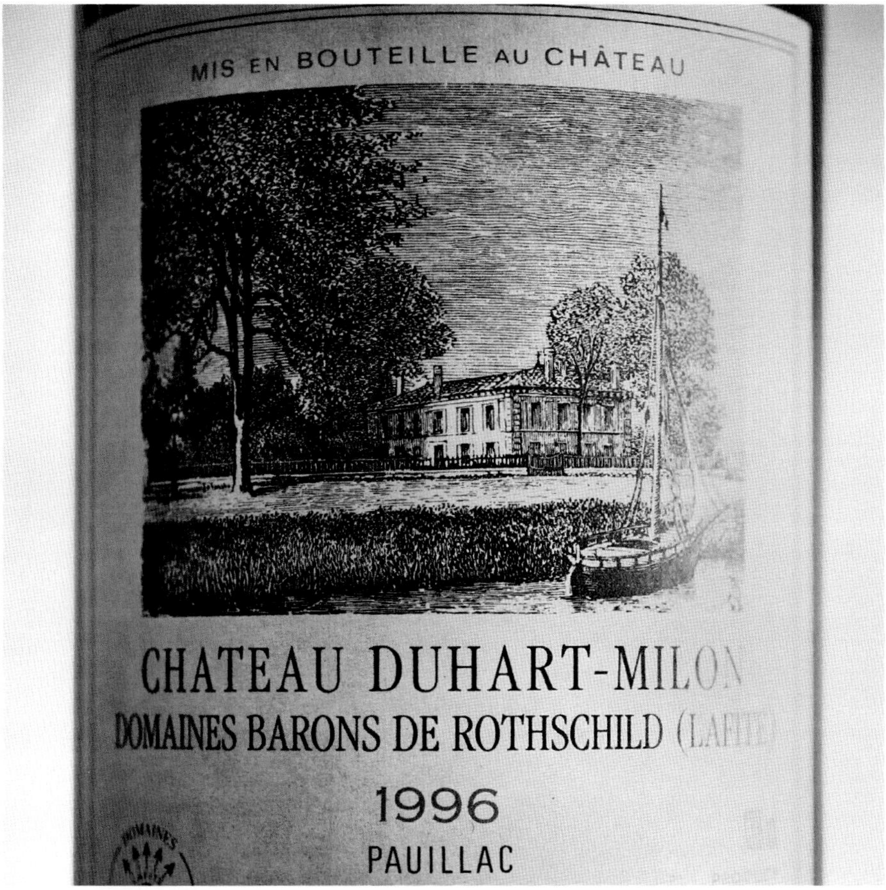

A Rothschild (but a much more affordable one) from Pat Baude's cellar.

still find expensive bad wine anywhere. Buying famous labels in warehouse stores is just one kind of lottery. If you don't like to gamble, the surest thing is to go to Tutto Bène, taste a wine you like and bring it home. That's another improvement over the "good old days"; there was nothing resembling a wine bar here forty years ago.

For the sake of economic science, last week I decided to test my optimism about today's wines. That Lafite that disappointed in 1967 was a cabernet, so I opened a 2003 Pavilion cabernet from Napa that also cost $15 (not adjusted for inflation) and got a delicious, juicy wine with bright cherry freshness—not complex or profound, sure, but a charming drink. To match the Bernkasteler, I found a Schloss Saarstein Riesling for $12. A fragrant, delicate wine with bittersweet stony depths, it may be too ethereal to pair with everyday food, but it was a perfect match for Sarah McLachlan's beautiful, sad new CD, *Wintersong*. Unlike that long-ago bottle of Bernkasteler, the Saarstein turned out to be unforgettable.

In addition to these contemporary bargains from well-known areas in California and Germany, there are even better deals from countries that were marginal producers only twenty years ago. For $8, pick up the whimsically named Wrongo Dongo and you'll taste a rich, red Spanish wine from monastrell grapes, full of plum and other dark fruit flavors, a good way to chase the winter blues. From South Africa, formerly off limits for so many reasons, try Ken Forrester's bracing white wine from chenin blanc grapes. The 2006, for just under $10, has a scent of ginger marmalade and tastes, well, cool.

So I've got it made these days—and I will continue to, so long as Indiana University believes that modern may be well and good but there's no substitute for a properly aged professor.

No Need to Show Off When Ordering Wine

(April/May 2007)

Critics of capitalism sometimes struggle for evidence that Adam Smith was wrong in his assumption that consumers will always choose the lowest price. Really, they need look no further than the usual restaurant's wine list. Even Masters of the Universe, who look for efficiencies in every other arena, will order overpriced wine just so they won't look cheap.

A few years ago, I was charged with feeding a distinguished visitor. We took her to a local restaurant that seemed to consider itself the best in town. (This was before Restaurant Tallent opened, so maybe it just was.) To start, I chose a Spanish Albariño, almost always a clean, fresh, stimulating bargain. The waiter grappled awkwardly with the cork and then announced pointedly that it was "hard to open these cheap wines."

A good restaurant, or a restaurant with a good wine list—the same thing, in my opinion—will strive to offer lots of bargains. In France, the Michelin Guide inspectors are said to order the house wine in simple restaurants, on the theory that any moron can sell good wine for 200 euros but a good restaurateur will take the trouble to find one to offer for a tenth as much. Here in Bloomington, I usually have good luck at places where the chef's intentions about his food are obvious. Such a chef is likely to take the trouble to find a group of affordable wines that will express the soul of the menu. Two restaurants just off the downtown Square come to mind.

Pricey bottles on the wine list of a San Francisco restaurant.

Janko's Little Zagreb is unmistakably dedicated to the carnal pleasures of indecently large, grilled slabs of red meat and consuming them with honest wines. Sure, the wine list offers any passing millionaire his shot at the conspicuous consumption of trophy wines like Opus One. It also offers the rest of us some plain delicious choices. My favorite right now is Valentin Bianchi's Malbec from Argentina—a tart, intense wine, almost black with dark flavors like blackberry and licorice ($30). Argentina, the only country where malbec grapes consistently make first-class wine, is also the only country whose average residents eat more than 150 pounds of beef per year. This is no coincidence. However, if I had a dinner companion too refined to be totally into the caveman red meat/black wine thing, I could be happy sharing Penfold's Bin 389 Cabernet Shiraz, a rich purple Australian blend with a somewhat more familiar international style ($38). (Though I would hope said companion would refrain from citing the steak-house cliché, "Cab and Cow.")

The Uptown Café offers a different but equally personal cooking style: lively and spicy Cajun dishes, many based on seafood. Here, too, the chef's taste in food drives the wine list. Fish wants wine that works like a slice of lemon. A sauvignon blanc from the Loire, Salvard Cheverny is just the thing—with the color of straw, the scent of a meadow and the bite of grapefruit ($25). The layers of flavor in the meat dishes call for a complex red wine, and Spanish Abadia Retuerta is a good fit, with almost spicy red fruit flavors, a rich texture and a solid quality ($36). Gordon Gekko might be inclined to spend a lot more money when choosing his wine, but he wouldn't drink as well.

(Summer + Wine = Happiness)

(June/July 2007)

"Wine," Benjamin Franklin wrote to French economist Abbé Morellet in 1779, is "a constant proof that God loves us, and loves to see us happy." The connoisseur who lies awake worrying whether his 1996 white Burgundies are oxidizing prematurely (probably) or whether his in-laws appreciated the Chateau Tirecul La Gravière (probably not) is missing the point. These decompressed early summer days in Bloomington are the best time to drink wine just to be happy.

Prosecco is a great choice for the season. This sparkling wine, made in the area around Venice, is often recommended as an inexpensive substitute for Champagne. It is a poor substitute, lacking racy minerality, tiny beads of perpetual bubbles or complex yeasty flavors like nuts or buttered brioche. But Champagne is also a poor substitute for prosecco, lacking its creamy bubbles and its fresh taste of citrus and white fruits like bananas, apples and pears.

I remember sitting in a bar across from the cathedral in Montagnana where a funeral was evidently in progress. As the bell tolled, six workmen at a table took off their woolen caps and lifted a glass of prosecco to the departed. Now there's a send-off Dr. Franklin would have appreciated!

The best prosecco is the freshest. The wine is not vintage-dated, so just go to a trusted, busy store and ask what prosecco is newest. The last time I did this at Big Red, I left with a $13 Collalbrigo Brut. It made me happy.

Toasting the summer with prosecco.

You can use the prosecco to make a Bellini, the easygoing, celebrated Venetian aperitif, by mixing one part peach puree to two parts prosecco. The drink is named after the Venetian painter, who favored a golden pink shade for nudes, sunsets and robes. Getting the right shade for the drink requires white peaches, which surprisingly often have some vivid red streaks in their flesh. To duplicate the original here, you can order frozen puree from Perfect Puree of Napa Valley, the supplier for most top-flight Italian restaurants in this country. Cheaper Italian restaurants often use peach margarita mix, which is way too sweet and has sour off-flavors. (Unfortunately, Perfect Puree requires a minimum shipment of sixty-six ounces.) Best of all, wait until our local peaches are perfectly ripe, puree them with a few strawberries and don't hold your drink up to a Venetian sunset for comparison. It's summertime; just be happy.

The other easy choice for the season is sangria. Authentic, original Spanish sangria was probably mediocre wine mixed with limonada. For the modern version, slice an orange and a lemon (local peaches work too) and then peel and chop a tart apple like an early local Jonathan and combine the fruit with the juice of another orange, a half cup of sweet liqueur, a bottle of Spanish wine and lots of ice. For the wine, I like $7 Borsao at Sahara Mart, and for the liqueur, a Spanish import called Cuarente y Tres from Big Red (Cointreau works just fine too).

Better yet, make the idea of sangria into a gorgeous cocktail. Boil the wine down by half and dissolve into it four tablespoons of sugar. Cool the resulting syrup, then combine one ounce with one ounce of Cointreau, two ounces of vodka, a squeeze of lemon juice and ice, and shake. Call it a "sangrini" if you like, but to me, it's Franklin's Punch.

Here's to Beer!

(August/September 2007)

Are you thirsty?

Sometimes you just want a beer. I'm not talking about after mowing the lawn in August, when anything wet will do, and I'm certainly not talking about at a keg party. I'm talking about those times when we want something refreshing but reassuring, something adult but not difficult, something supportive, familiar and connected with the positive side of civilization.

During Prohibition, you could still get whiskey from your doctor or wine from your rabbi. But beer was completely forbidden. Maybe beer had to be banned because it so clearly demonstrated the honest pleasure of drinking. The Supreme Court said it lacked "any substantial value." The court was talking about medical value, but once Prohibition ended in 1933, it seems as if the giants of the American brewing industry were also determined to make sure beer lacked any taste value as well.

Happily, smaller local brewers are filling the gap. There are two first-rate ones in Bloomington. The Bloomington Brewing Company, for example, has made Quarrymen Pale Ale since the mid-1990s. Unfiltered, copper-colored and less fizzy than mass-market beer, the Quarrymen has the distinctive floral flavor of Cascade hops from the West Coast and a slight bitterness. This typical American microbrew is a fine match for brightly flavored "pub grub."

The Bloomington Brewing Company and Lennie's, serving beer, pizza and more.

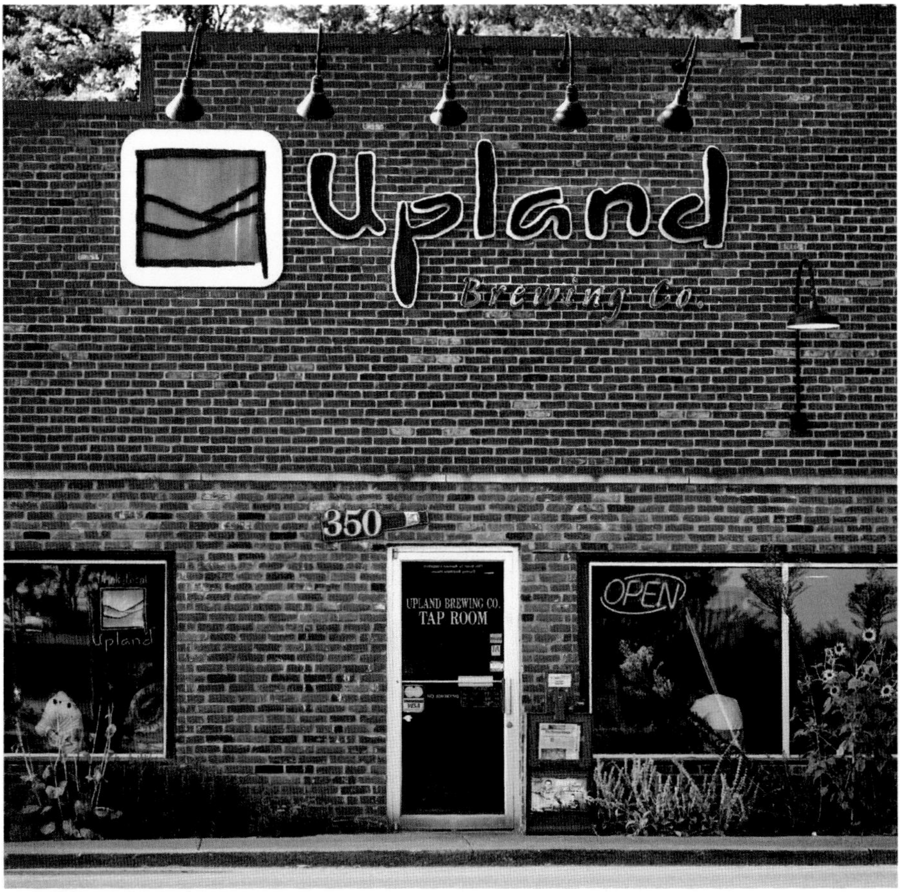

The Upland Brewing Company, open for beer and dinner on a summer night.

The taps of delicious beer at the Upland Brewing Company.

The other local choice is the Upland Brewing Company. Its light, tart, refreshing wheat beer is an antidote for the steaming heat of Bloomington's late summer and is perfect with the chilled seafood that I hope to see on my plate in this weather. I also like Upland's Dragonfly India Pale Ale. This style of beer was originally loaded with alcohol and bitter hops to fortify it for the journey from England to India. The association with India sometimes brings IPA to the table with really spicy food—a mistake. High alcohol, burning spices and steamy heat are not my idea of a good time, even if the Upland is not as alcoholic or bitter as some versions. What this ale wants to do for you is to cut through richness. Make some fried chicken, serve it at room temperature with an iced Dragonfly and you will see what hops can do for you.

These and other types of beer are served from the tap at the breweries, along with casual meals. You can also take home a draft jug, called a "growler." It's always fun to watch your beer-loving guests' eyes widen with anticipation when they see a whole fresh jug. Upland's beers are bottled conventionally as well and sold in stores. Best of all, go to Trulli Flatbread, where these local beers join some of the world's most interesting choices in an inspired beer list.

Wherever one finds good beer, the biggest mistake is to drink it solemnly. Of course it has alcohol and must be respected. Of course the skill and imagination of its brewer is a wondrous thing. Yet the joy to be had here is not sniffing, swirling, erudite criticism or snobbery. The point of getting together with a few friends and a few beers is to connect—with them and with the bounty of the earth. But if there's no singing involved, you may need better beer or cooler friends.

Some Events Deserve Champagne

(October/November 2007)

On my father's 100th birthday, five years ago, we opened a Mumm's Cordon Rouge. This delicate Champagne was a lifelong favorite of his, although I would choose something a little richer for my own century mark. Still, it was a lovely evening that would have been even happier had he not died eighteen years earlier. The point remains that some memories and some events deserve Champagne.

A lot of Champagne, definitely including expensive French bottlings, is no more than handsomely labeled overpriced wine. The basic products of the "Big Brands" (les Grandes Marques) are industrial wines, usually blended from wines produced by growers throughout the region, based less on grapes and soil than on witty, beautiful lifestyle ads in magazines like *Vogue*, *Gourmet* or the *New Yorker*. They are designed to sell for around $30 a bottle, often sweetened for a marketplace more accustomed to iced colas. The appeal of these branded bottles is the same as a double mocha latte: unable to swing real luxuries like yachts and Bentleys, we can buy a small treat and fantasize the rest.

There is an important trick to this market, however. For only a few dollars more than big-brand, eye-candy Champagne, you can get some really delicious stuff. There are two ways to go. My own favorites are the wines of individual artisanal growers, known as "farmer fizz" to fans. These wines

A picture of Pat Baude's father, André, and a glass of André's favorite Champagne. *Photo of André from a family collection.*

are not much advertised, not made by the millions, not sweetened. They are lovely examples of individual decisions by small growers in distinctive vineyards. I have recently had two from Big Red. For $48, the Gimonnet Cuis has a floral scent, a flavor of citrus fruit mixed with a hint of minerals (the way clean gravel smells in the rain) and a tantalizing herbal note at the end. For $2 more, Pierre Peters Brut has obvious minerals and a gingery fruity tang.

Apart from farmer fizz, the second way to go is with a small producer rather than a mass-market brand. At Restaurant Tallent, for example, Moet White Label is available for those who want a standard brand for $68. For just $7 more, you can be drinking a delightful Deutz. Deutz was a family firm bought out by the big brand Roederer, makers of Cristal, the favorite $200 Champagne of rap stars. But Roederer lets Deutz continue in its own old ways, making a rich Champagne whose substantial flavors run more to apples and pears than citrus, with yeasty flavors like toast in place of minerality—a perfect match to Dave Tallent's scallops. Henriot is another small firm with exceptional wines, sometimes on the list at Tallent.

Okay, I know, these $50 and $75 bottles are not as affordable luxuries as a quick trip to Starbucks. But they are true luxuries in a way that standard Champagne is not. Yeah, Catherine Zeta-Jones is easy to look at and easy to find at a theater near you, but Julie Delpy is a great actress and worth looking for. While you're looking, stop by Sahara Mart to pick up a bottle of Canella Prosecco for less than $15. This fresh and zippy Italian sparkling wine will lift everybody's mood, even if it's not right for a 100th birthday.

Beaujolais: Unappreciated and a Bargain

(December 2007/January 2008)

I was fortunate to have a week on the northern California coast in late October. Aside from the waves and redwoods and sea mammals, I spent some time with pinot noirs from the Russian River valley.

For my money, these rich, fruity, powerful wines are as interesting as any in the world. But on day six, in a French-hippie fusion restaurant oddly called Café Beaujolais in Mendocino, it struck me how un-Californian these weighty pinots are. California and its table are based on the lightness of being and are not well matched with the gravitas of these deep wines. What California needs but doesn't grow itself is a wine like Beaujolais.

Beaujolais may be the most underappreciated wine outside France and is therefore a great bargain. True, ordinary Beaujolais is no more exciting than a number of wines routinely available in Bloomington for around $10. Beaujolais is made from gamay grapes grown north of Lyon, near the costly and famous Burgundian pinot noir vineyards. This fresh, simple wine is mainly a counterpoint to the spicy sausages and stinky cheeses of the region. Portions of the area are allowed to call their wines by the slightly more restrictive name of Beaujolais-Villages, meaning that they cost a couple of dollars more and might have a recognizable scent of red berries and an earthy undertone.

Pinot noir grapes in the Russian River Valley.

A close-up of pinot noir grapes.

Spend a few dollars more (at Bloomington prices, from the high teens to the high twenties), and you can buy one of the "crus." These wines are a different world. They come from Beaujolais and have the legal right to call themselves by that name, but they mostly don't deign to use the name. They simply call themselves by the name of one of the ten communes where they are made.

The commune names we are likely to see in Bloomington are Moulin-à-Vent, Morgon, Fleurie or Côte de Brouilly. From Sahara Mart, for example, try the Morgon made by Foillard. The color is bright crimson, the scent a bouquet of mixed flowers, the texture pure silk. The first taste is of strawberries, but what lingers afterward is raspberry. Compare the Fleurie from Chignard at Big Red. When I tasted this without seeing the label, my first thought was pinot from Burgundy, but a particularly fresh and spicy version. At Restaurant Tallent, order the Côte de Brouilly by Chanrion, floral with an earthy note, a beautiful match for the vegetarian pasta or almost anything from the sprightly new bar menu.

The importer Kermit Lynch has long worked at bringing in the best examples of these charmers, and Cédric Picard, wine guru at Big Red, persuaded Lynch to send in some advance samples. (I guess I should respect his ethnicity and refer to Cédric as a savant rather than guru.) First the '05s. First a Thévenet, Morgon Vielles Vignes. The nose had a deep background scent, which everybody liked, and another element that people characterized with descriptors ranging from funky to barnyard to worse. I liked it and also liked the thick flavors of cherry, almond and vanilla. Not for the faint of heart, anyway. On the other hand, the Guy Breton Morgon was a beautiful violet wine with a wonderful bouquet of flowers (finally justifying the word) and a light but pleasant taste of red berries—a good choice for those put off by the earthiness of the Thévenet. Then the '06s. First a Dupeuple Beaujolais, a simple wine with a slight note of bubble gum. It reminded me of cherry cough drops, but good cherry cough drops. Then a more serious wine, a Thivin Côte de Brouilly, with a silky texture, maybe red currant more than cherry, and a lingering spicy note. I was disappointed in the Diochon Moulin-à-Vent, usually a more impressive wine but tonight shallow and short. Finally a real winner, the Domaine Chignard's Fleurie "Les Moriers." The powerful fruits climbed right out of the glass; no need to bury the geeky nose in the glass for this one. The liquid coats the mouth and perfumes it for a good while afterward. I thought at first that this was an impostor, that a pinot noir from Beaune had been slipped in to test us. I think the bottom line is that '06 will both require and reward careful buying.

A different matter altogether is "Beaujolais nouveau." This is a frivolous wine marketed extensively by big commercial houses. Released around the world on the third Thursday of every November, the wine is made from September's harvest. It has little depth and, thanks to quick-acting yeasts, tastes a little like bananas or bubble gum. Major growers blame the nouveau for Beaujolais' limited reputation and resulting low price. Maybe so. But sometime in this season's gray drizzle, I plan to stop by Tutto Bène for a reminder of summer's playfulness. If once a year you can't get a kick out of a note of bubble gum in a glass, life has become too solemn.

[Editor's note: For more on Beaujolais nouveau, see page 149.]

Intriguing Wines for $8 to $18

(February/March 2008)

A publisher friend of mine is a man of advanced aesthetic sensibilities, a lover of music and the arts, a devotee of the theater, a man who has mastered typeface, the rhythm of the English language and the look of a great photograph. But wine is not his "thing." We were listening to jazz over a glass of vernacchia at Tutto Bène one evening. Hoping to interest him in an article I was planning about the wine, I pointed out that it was grown in San Gimignano, where Zeffirelli's film *Tea with Mussolini* ends. He was immediately fascinated and dissected the film's faults thoroughly. We never got back to the wine.

At a meeting over pizza at his house, he asked me to pick a wine from his wine rack, stocked with good sensible bottles. I chose a Bolla Valpolicella that seemed to please everyone. At the time, though, I thought that someday I would write a column about how, in Bloomington, for the same money as the wines in that rack, one could put together a collection of less familiar but more intriguing wines. This column is my effort to find a few wines between $8 and $18, wines you could open just because you felt like it but also wines that would repay careful attention.

I'd start with two screaming bargains under $10 at Sahara Mart. The 2006 Borsao is a bright Spanish wine with solid, dark cherry flavor and a hint of anise. The 2006 La Vieille Ferme blanc is a dry white wine from Provence, suggesting lemon zest and grapefruit (got sushi?).

The wide variety of wines available at the Sahara Mart.

Even more wine at Sahara Mart.

For a special treat, try one of "Manolo's Wines." Manuel Hernandez-Martin, based in Bloomington, directly imports a portfolio of organic wines from small Spanish producers. His 2006 Clos del Pinell blanc is a not-quite-bone-dry white from Terra Alta, with scents of peach and pear—an amazing match for kung pao shrimp. Ever since the movie *Sideways*, marketers have produced a lot of coarsened versions of cheap pinot noir. One of the few affordable but still elegant choices is the 2005 A-to-Z from Oregon, smiling, spicy and full of gentle berry flavors.

At Big Red, try the 2005 Saumur from Cave de Saumur. This is a specially imported wine for Big Red, unavailable, so far as I know, elsewhere in the United States. Made in France from chenin blanc grapes, the result is a golden wine with floral aromas and a teasing bitter taste—perfection with most soft cheeses. For a more conventional white, Verget's 2006 Macon Villages shows that chardonnay can make a clean wine with crisp slate-like flavors. For reds, the 2005 Mas de Gourgonnier is a ripe and easygoing blend of Rhône grapes, just the thing to accompany a bone-warming winter dish, especially one with some beans and garlic in it. And the 2006 Bitch, despite the Australian frat-boy name, is another friendly wine that brings a definite touch of warmth with its lively grenache flavors.

So, will my publishing friend heed any of my advice? He did once drink some prosecco and told me he really liked it. Of course he was honeymooning in Venice, and under those circumstances, even Faygo Red Pop is nectar of the gods.

For Good Advice, Ask at Big Red and Sahara Mart

(April/May 2008)

I just read a review of a 2004 Barolo that described its flavor as "sexy smoke and saline earth." I can enjoy imagining sexy smoke—I think of Carla Bruni (the model/new wife of French prime minister Nicolas Sarkozy) and a Gauloise. Saline earth is harder for me, as I don't usually salt my dirt before eating it. Something like this probably led University of Chicago economist Roman Weil to publish a recent experiment in which he asked experienced wine drinkers to distinguish between two $50 Bordeaux by reading noted expert Robert Parker's published descriptions of their flavor. It turns out they would have done slightly better just guessing.

Still, almost all of us wine lovers can be seen at some time in the store, clutching *Wine Spectator* magazine or, worse, connecting to Robert Parker's website by Java-enabled cellphone, picking a flavor of cassis, licorice and spicy leather, or perhaps stony minerals with high-toned yellow fruit and coarse-ground white pepper. It's time to take a deep breath and realize that the people who stock the store should be the front line for advice. If not, go someplace else.

Try Big Red, for example. This has become the best collection of wine in Indiana. Thanks to past efforts by Patrick Mitten and Cédric Picard, there are thousands of wines and a tradition of staff experts who can tell you about them. Both Patrick and Cédric have recently left Big Red. Bobby Wallace and Bobby DerOhanian are now in charge.

William Baude, experimenting (unsuccessfully) with the taste of "saline dirt."

Wallace was the sommelier at Peterson's in Indianapolis, and DerOhanian worked at Restaurant Tallent in Bloomington. Twice I have asked Wallace for a wine recommendation to match a particular dish, and twice he ended up giving me a little cooking lesson to make my dish match the wine. I have learned a lot from him. Did you know you can make a pork chop taste slightly smoky by rubbing the grill with a small bit of oil, letting the oil burn for a few seconds and putting the meat right on the spot? It matches the faint smokiness of a Valsacro Rioja, aged in charred barrels, and I hope Ms. Bruni will like it.

Cédric Picard will remain in Bloomington until the summer, working as a consultant for Sahara Mart, which is opening a new store on East Third Street. He has been charged to make this the best collection in southern Indiana.

The resulting competition can only be good for the consumer. The different backgrounds of Wallace (American, restaurant sommelier) and Picard (French, winemaking experience) show in their approaches to choosing and suggesting wine. Americans think of wine by grape variety, and Big Red recently arranged a very American tasting—all from merlot grapes but from different places in Washington, Umbria, California, Australia and both banks of the Gironde River in Bordeaux. Europeans, on the other hand, think of terroir rather than varietal, and Sahara Mart offered a tasting of artisanal wines made in Champagne from combinations of three different grapes. To Walace's six different merlots, I added two older Europeans from my cellar. We bothered Dave Tallent for a few delicious appetizers and sat down with wine manager DerOhanian to see what we thought.

I found three wines to like. We all liked a wine from Washington, the 2003 Northstar for $28. This was a fresh, spicy wine with a bold blackberry flavor and hints of mocha. It seems to be common in recent tastings around the country for Washington merlots to outclass those from California. Merlot ripens easily, and things (grapes, plots, politics) that ripen easily anywhere else can quickly become overripe in California. The Northstar kept its freshness well. I also liked the Chateau Bon Pasteur 2000, from my cellar. This large, complex Bordeaux wine from Pomerol has a thick texture and rich fruit—but it would clearly have been better if it had stayed in the cellar for another few years. My third pick, and a real bargain at $20, was the Chateau Suau 2005, a nicely balanced lighter Bordeaux, suggesting plums and cherries.

The Sahara Mart (in its original location).

Big Red Liquors has a wide array of wine in addition to other things to drink.

I was put off by the one Australian example, the 2006 Mollydooker "Scooter" for $20. It smelled like candied fruit, felt a little like syrup and tasted too much like vodka for me. A true Mollydooker—strong feelings, positive or negative, pretty much guaranteed. The two Californians, Shafer 2005 for $55 and 2004 Jarvis for $75, were well-made, suave and polished wines—but I found them a bit dull. They lacked the depth of the Pomerol on the one hand while also failing to bring the uplifting freshness of the Northstar or the Suau to the table. My Italian contribution, the 1998 Montiano, was weedy and uninteresting. This wine has a considerable following, but I'd never had it before. It may just have been a bad bottle. Another French wine, Chateau L'Ecuyer for $43, was a little funky in the nose and somewhat brambly in the mouth. Perhaps it will settle down in a few years and repay cellaring, but with a tasty Chateau Suau for less than half the price, I won't be the one to find out.

It seems impossible to talk about the red wine made from merlot grapes without quoting Miles's line from the film *Sideways*: "If anyone orders merlot, I'm leaving. I'm not drinking any fucking merlot." Since the film was released in 2004, the consumption of merlot has declined some, and the price has definitely plummeted. One irony of the price drop is that we may all be drinking more merlot than ever but without knowing it. An American wine labeled simply by grape, say cabernet, can actually contain up to 25 percent of a different variety. The production of merlot grapes has not declined as much as the consumption of merlot wine, a pattern that, when combined with the lower price for merlot, suggests that it may have become a filler for other varietals. It would be a splendid irony if Miles's beloved pinot noirs are now made of 25 percent merlot—and given the increased flow of undistinguished pinot since the movie, there could well be a lot of things lurking in these bottles.

What do I think about Miles's dictum now? Merlot is easy to make and usually turns out okay. It happened to be just coming into visibility in California in 1991, the year the CBS documentary on the *French Paradox* was pushing the idea that red wine will save your heart. A lot of folks in America decided to replace their ubiquitous cheap bar glasses of chardonnay with something red. Merlot was easy to grow, easy to drink, easy to pronounce and good for you besides. Too much was planted, too much drunk, too much of it dull and sweet, as befits a cheap bar drink. It was already losing its appeal when Miles dispatched it. But good merlot remains a fine wine indeed, and I will be looking for mine in the state of Washington and from Pomerol, on the right bank of the river by Bordeaux.

Wines for Those Lazy, Hazy, Crazy Days of Summer

(June/July 2008)

These summer days make me cheap and lazy. The lazy part shows in my idea of a summer meal, which is to go down to the farmers' market, buy what looks good and pile it all on an outdoor grill for a while. If company's coming, I might remember to add salt and pepper and even some olive oil. The cheap part leads me to avoid wines from the Napa Valley and anywhere the price is figured in euros.

The cheap and the lazy work well together. Grilling gives food an appetizing bitterness, but the bitterness is likely to clash with the tannins resulting from serious aging in oak barrels—about the only way they make wine these days in Napa Valley. And the primal flavors of the grill can be awkward with the balance and complexity inherent in traditional euro-zone winemaking. This is a good time to explore wines from the rest of the New World, especially malbecs from Argentina and unoaked chardonnays from Australia.

The malbec grape used to be grown in several parts of France, where it makes at best a dark and intense red wine but is more often slow to ripen before the frost and likely to turn out hard and ungenerous. In Argentina, on the other hand, it flourishes on the eastern slopes of the Andes, ripening easily during a long season in full sunlight but retaining fresh and fruity qualities thanks to cool temperatures at several thousand feet above sea

Piling summer's bounty on the grill.

Cornfields near Bloomington in the summer.

level. Until fifteen years ago, Argentine wines were often produced with little effort and care, sold mainly in Argentina to wash down the national dish of grilled steak. Recently, local growers have cleaned up their act and taken full advantage of the natural advantages of their sites, including freedom from the need to use herbicides and pesticides.

By the way, 2006 seems to have been the best year for malbec ever. There are serious malbecs in town for $60 or more, but my own favorites are between $10 and $12 a bottle. Altos Las Hermigas has a beautiful purple color, smells of flowers and berries and fills the mouth with rich, clean flavors. Equally satisfying is Pascual Toso, which is a touch spicier.

When meat is not a big part of the mix, especially as the summer's vegetables grow richer and sweeter, I find an Australian chardonnay without oak can be revealing. If you think chardonnay tastes buttery or caramelized, you've been drinking Californian wines flavored with French oak. French chardonnay, for that matter, is either heavily influenced by oak or, as in Chablis, is racy and bone-dry. Neither one is a good match for corn, peppers, tomatoes or other sweet, smoky vegetables.

Unoaked Australian chardonnay, on the other hand, is full of pure fruit flavors—pear, pineapple, citrus and even mango. If bottled simply and inexpensively without long aging in heavy oak, the result is a charming lift for simple vegetables. You can find several different versions of Australian chardonnay marked "unoaked." I like them all, but my favorite is Tapestry, for about $12.

Sahara Mart and Big Red both carry all these wines. The main trouble finding them is that they are remarkable bargains and hard to keep on the shelves.

The Great International Debate You Can Test at Home

(August/September 2008)

Critics of conductor Herbert von Karajan claim that, in answer to a taxi driver's "Where to, Maestro?" he replied, "It doesn't matter. I am in demand everywhere." Karajan's global popularity, with his brisk tempos and silken strings, has sometimes been blamed for submerging creativity and individuality in shimmering sound. Some wine lovers complain that contemporary wine has undergone a similar globalization, tasting the same from almost everywhere, fruity and smooth, with a shimmering taste that buries the distinctions of different vineyards and the traditions of different cultures.

International style depends on the use of well-known grape varieties, aging in small oak barrels and malolactic fermentation, which converts tart apple flavor to something more like sweet butter. Enemies of international style in wine admire Jonathan Nossiter's art-house documentary film *Mondovino* (now on DVD). The style's defenders are looking forward instead to the theatrical release in October of *Bottle Shock*, starring Alan Rickman, which glorifies the 1976 blind tasting in Paris when French wine experts appalled themselves by preferring California wines to Bordeaux.

For once, here is a debate in aesthetic philosophy that you can taste. Go to Tutto Bène and order two glasses of wine. First, a moschofilero, grown only in Greece. It has a powerful floral perfume and a gentle melon-like flavor. This wine has never seen an oaken barrel and won't remind you of any other

Comparing two glasses of wine at the bar at Tallent (Tutto Bène has closed).

wine you know—unless you have visited Peloponnesus. Second, order some Conundrum, a California wine made from a blend of grapes dominated by the international favorites, chardonnay and sauvignon blanc, and then aged in oak. This, too, is a good drink, but it will show the creamy texture and spicy vanilla flavor of oak aging and a little butter.

Or try this at home. From Big Red, buy two California wines: Kendall Jackson chardonnay reserve and Tangent pinot blanc. The Kendall Jackson has rich pineapple and coconut flavors, oaky spice and butter. The Tangent, from a less familiar grape, is lighter, more apple than pineapple, with no oak or butter. The chardonnay seems familiar even if I couldn't place it in Australia, California, Chile or South Africa. This pinot blanc, on the other hand, seems unique; the same grape in Italy makes a delightfully frivolous wine, in Oregon a sharper one and in Alsace, a wine with more mineral and less fruit.

You can conduct the same test with red wine. From Sahara Mart, try Clos de la Siete, from Argentina, a persuasive argument for the international style—rich black fruit, smoky oak highlights, smooth texture, made from a blend of grapes including international favorites cabernet sauvignon and merlot as well as the Argentinean star, malbec. Contrast the Bourgueil from Chanteleuserie, an unoaked wine made in France's Loire Valley from cabernet franc grapes, with a jump-out-of-the-glass rush of fresh berries and herbs.

Like the French experts in 1976, you could try tasting these wines blind. Proponents of the international style recommend this as the ultimate test of quality; it is also a good teacher of humility. Defenders of local terroir reply that wine should be evaluated in its context and by the particular aspirations of its makers. Personally, I side with Kermit Lynch, importer of the Bourgueil, who says that blind tasting is to wine as strip poker is to love.

Will It Be Beer or Wine (or Both) This Thanksgiving?

(October/November 2008)

The Pilgrims were bound for Virginia when they had to stop at Plymouth Rock, "our victuals being pretty much spent especially our beer." That explains why our traditional meal celebrating their first harvest matches beer better than wine. No one wine can complement spicy cranberries, creamed onions and cornbread—and the only thing I have ever found to drink with candied sweet potatoes and marshmallows is Coca-Cola.

Those who dream of the original intent of the founders, say Supreme Court Justice Antonin Scalia, had better limit themselves to beer on Thanksgiving. In Bloomington, this could be a pleasant duty. Both local brewers, Upland and Bloomington Brewing Company, make fine beers. Decking the harvest table with a variety of them would be a welcoming sight of historicism. Although cider was probably not made until the second Thanksgiving, I would add Oliver Winery's Beanblossom hard cider—a semisweet way to celebrate the bounty of our own local harvest and an outstanding example of how good real cider can be.

But if we think of Thanksgiving as an evolving present-day holiday and remember that the United States is now the second-largest consumer of wine in the world, we may want some wine on the table. If your table is large and the menu traditional with wine-killers like cranberry relish and sweet potatoes, the answer is La Vielle Ferme, a French wine delicious in

Original intent versus evolving standards: beer or wine?

red or white, widely available for about $7. The white is dry with notes of flowers and citrus, distinctive enough to stand up to the side dishes but sufficiently restrained to keep the peace with turkey. The red is deep with dark fruity flavors, easy to drink with rich food. Have both on the table. There is a reason this is the house wine at FARMBloomington and that Andrew Myers, the respected sommelier of Washington's CityZen, recently described his home refrigerator to wine writer Lettie Teague by saying, "I fill it up with bottles of La Vielle Ferme…dirt cheap…and yummy." If Uncle Frank complains the wine is cheap, tell him to bring all the Krug Champagne he wants.

In our home, as the table grows smaller and I am unwilling to spend precious time with my visiting children messing with pie crust or assembling vegetable casseroles, Thanksgiving has been streamlined to a normal-sized meal featuring a really good turkey. This, unlike the full feast for a huge cast, is the right time to bring out a special bottle.

Turkey itself is a great friend of wine, especially if the bird is free-ranged by a local farmer or an heirloom variety. Either a white or red wine would work. For white, I'd pick an Austrian grüner veltliner. At either Sahara Mart or Big Red, ask for advice about their grüners. Both stores have a changing selection from the low teens to about $60. They're all good. For a red, say with chestnut or sausage stuffing, I would find it hard to choose between a rich Qupé 2005 Bien Nacido Syrah from Sahara Mart ($25) and a lively Ponzi Willamette pinot noir 2006 at Big Red ($34)—or any other 2006 pinot noir from Oregon, a wonderful vintage, for which I certainly give thanks.

Can't-Miss Holiday Gifts: Pairings of Wine and Music

(December 2008/January 2009)

Trust me on this. No adult ever exchanges a bottle of Burgundy for a necktie with a heartrending picture of a spaniel. If your holiday involves finding a gift for a wine lover, don't complicate your life. A bottle of real Champagne, a half-case of mixed modest Spanish table wine, a bottle of your favorite or her favorite—all will be welcome and all will be used gratefully.

The same cannot be said for most wine gadgets or picturesque trays, aprons or the like. The one exception here is a real Laguiole corkscrew. These are handmade, exquisite to hold, old-fashioned tools, intended not so much for those who crave the newest iPhones as for someone who admires the craftsmanship of an English shotgun. Beware widespread second-rate models from France as well as China. Goods for Cooks has some of the best—not cheap at $150 or a little more, but this represents a savings of about £4,900 sterling on the shotgun.

If a bottle of wine seems unimaginative by itself, you can take an idea from the German wine aristocrats. In the castles of the Rhine, it was not uncommon to serve water with the evening meal and only afterward open the great wine with suitable music. You could treat your friend like a Graf and give him some wine and music together. Start with almost any 2007 German Riesling—the best year in recent memory. Excellent examples of the vintage are just now arriving in Bloomington from Valckenberg, an

A Laguiole corkscrew and its victim.

importer that offers good value at every price level. Match the wine with any Schubert disk from the Beaux Arts Trio.

If this seems excessively Teutonic, you can make it Italian. From the new Sahara Mart, pick one of several selections of Amarone. This is a rich and warm Italian wine made near Venice from partly raisined grapes, an example of what Italians call a wine for meditazione rather than dinner. The Masi would be my choice. Accompany it with any Puccini at all, but ideally Maria Callas singing "Vissi d'arte," and at the end of the day you should be rewarded with some teary kisses. If this whole experience seems too Mediterranean, you can also create a hometown version. Start with Oliver Winery's ice wine, a rich sweet essence that has enough tart fruit to be refreshing rather than cloying. Pair it with music from a favorite Lotus World Festival performer—for me, that would be "Cuilidh" from Julie Fowlis.

If you're concerned that giving wine still seems too obvious, you can push the idea with a cutting-edge distilled spirit. Now that single-malt whiskey has become familiar (although unfortunately neither commonplace nor affordable), trendsetters are turning to artisanal gin. The most interesting of these, available at Big Red, is Junipero, one of the projects for which the distiller, washing-machine heir Fritz Maytag, recently received the 2008 Lifetime Achievement Award from the James Beard Foundation. This gin has a penetrating piney quality accented by citrus and warm spices like cinnamon and cardamom. Purists sip it from a brandy snifter at room temperature (yech!), but philistines like me use it for the definitive martini. In either case, it is an exact match for Oscar Peterson's "Night Train."

How to Find Delightful Wines for $10 or Less

(February/March 2009)

The easiest way to get a boring $10 meal is to go to any highly advertised chain restaurant and order something cheap. For a good $10 dinner, go someplace local that specializes in the kind of food that is inexpensive by nature—you can score killer barbecue, pad thai or tamales. It's the same story shopping for wine. For mediocre, pick a big brand with lots of advertising and look for the $9.99 special. Good inexpensive wines come from small growers in obscure places (no Napa, no Bordeaux) made from lesser grape varieties (no pinot, no riesling).

As a test, I went to Sahara Mart and Big Red and asked for good wines under $10 from small growers. I came home with thirty bottles, invited friends over and started drinking. None of these wines were bad; some were strange, a couple were too old, most were interesting and a few were simply delicious.

There were three wines one could confidently serve at a dinner party for the boss, except that she might wonder if her staff were overpaid. One white wine struck a perfect balance—ordinary whites often either lack zest or hurt your mouth with sharp acids. Hugues Beaulieu's Coteaux du Languedoc from picpoul de pinet grapes ($8 at Big Red) combines floral and citrus flavors with just enough acid to refresh rather than bite the drinker. Languedoc, France's wine lake, is usually known more for

Piles of "killer barbeque" matched with a syrah.

quantity than fresh lively flavors. The picpoul is about as obscure a grape as there is.

Two red wines also showed beautifully. A 2006 petite sirah from Australia's De Bortoli ($8 at Sahara Mart) was a juicy wine with a scent of plums, a rich feeling in the mouth and a lingering, slightly spicy finish. Most wine drinkers recognize Australian shiraz, but the "petite sirah" is a completely different grape variety whose exact identity is in dispute. The 2006 El Ganador Argentinean malbec ($10 at Big Red) was a big and striking wine, with aromas of blackberries and tar and bracing flavors.

Wines like these certainly help the budget, illustrating my French grandmother's adage that "thrift is better than an annuity" (*mieux vaut règle que rente*). But knowledge as well as money can be gleaned from frugality. No one can appreciate food who always chooses foie gras over fried chicken. And I don't think the wine snob who limits himself to Napa cabernet has even begun to understand what wine is, to understand its enduring link between the earth and the table.

Expensive wines are alike in their smoothness, complexity, depth and predictability. That's what you pay for. But the joy of wine is that it can surprise and delight as well. I got a lot of both from this exercise. A Portuguese bottle from Sahara Mart (Restoration 2007), made in part from a grape I had never heard of, smelled like a new flower I have yet to meet. A farmers' cooperative wine from the South of France (Corbières Col des Vents 2005, Big Red) finally explained to me what other wine writers must mean by "earthiness." These insights may not be as good as an annuity, but they sure beat the stock market.

In 2001, Robert Parker's *Wine Advocate* listed several hundred value wines, all priced for less than $16 and some for as little as $5. In those days, I thought the only reason to spend $25 for a bottle was vanity or maybe curiosity. The 2008 *Advocate* now defines a value wine as one under $25. This week's *Wine Spectator* uses the $20 figure and lists a thousand value wines, of which exactly thirteen are under $10 (although another dozen or so are listed at exactly $10). But people in the business say that in the present mood of careful spending, many more people are asking for wines under $10. You'll see big displays in local stores of wines in that category.

Complete Tasting Notes: Wines marked with an * were ones I thought to be very good at any price. I wasn't bored or unhappy with any of them.

Vinum Africa, Chenin Blanc 2007. Rich and creamy wine from South Africa, with an appetizing bitterness. No hint of the special quince-like flavor of chenin blanc. A good match for slightly sweet vegetables like corn or winter squash.

Oxford Landing Grenache-Syrah-Mourvedre. Bright red Australian, tart with clean fresh fruit flavors, not smooth. Soak some oak chips in it and it would taste like what you get in cheap steakhouse chains, but it's much nicer with the freshness.

Cuvee de Pena 2005. A beautiful dark glowing color, good bite and a slight oxidative note, giving it a rustic feel, straight from the heart of darkest France. I liked it, but not everyone will enjoy the rough edges as I did. You can also buy this in a three-liter box for $30, which is both a good buy and kind to the environment.

Restoration 2007. A Portuguese wine with a reddish-black color, good body, lots of acid and a long finish of plums and cherries. Different and for sure worth trying.

Caposaldo Pinot Grigio 2007. Tastes like pinot grigio, but it's short on aromatics. Inoffensive, but I wouldn't buy it again.

*Hugues Beaulieu, Picpoul de Pinet 2007. Wow. Made of an obscure grape from Languedoc, this is a soft and seductive white wine with a sense of melons and a meadow. June in a glass.

Skouras White 2007. A Greek white wine, smooth with a nose of lemon drops. Not bad but a little heavy for my taste. This is a big firm, and I do like some of their pricier whites.

Black Wing Chardonnay Padthaway 2006. Made by a small Australian winery from purchased grapes. Gold color, bright pineapple flavor, pleasant but nothing special.

Jurschitsch Mozart Grüner Veltliner 2007. This is a "fun" wine made by one of the classical producers of classy GV in Austria. It's spicy, a little yeasty and fresh. It lacks the finesse and elegance of its big sisters, but it would brighten any meal. Try it with fried catfish for a nice kick.

*EL GANADOR MALBEC 2006. Absolutely everything you could ask of an Argentinian malbec. Big and purple, filling the mouth with black fruit and the nose with sweet flowers. Lingering aftertaste. If you eat red meat, you should have this wine.

MAIPO MALBEC 2007. Another good malbec from Argentina, refined, aromatic and full of blackberries.

VINEDOS EL SEQUE 2006. A Spanish wine from Alicante, made of Monastrell (Mourvedre) grapes. Big, fresh, purple color with lively red fruit flavors. A first-rate wine if you like some acid.

LA MANO BIERZO 2006. Made from Mencia grapes, pretty much unknown elsewhere, Bierzo wines are trendy and a favorite of hip sommeliers. This version, although not outstanding, shows you exactly why, with its bright red color and subtle blueberry-like flavor.

CELLERS UNIO, ROUREDA RUBI 2007. This Spanish rose, imported by Bloomington-based Manolo's Wines, is meatier and more substantial than most roses, based on half grenache and half merlot grapes. It is soft and floral and would be close to perfect if it had a little more acidity.

FIGARO CALATAYUD TINTO 2005. I'm snowed in as I write this, and this would be a good wine to be snowed in with. Deep red with black cherry notes and hints of spice and almonds, the long finish of this all-garnacha wine leaves a warm glow, helped along by 14.5 percent alcohol.

*DE BORTOLI DB PETITE SYRAH 2006. Petite syrah is a mysterious grape, and so far at least, DNA testing only adds to the mystery of what is called petite syrah around the world. But this is definitely a mystery to engage, and here is a sensational example. Deep plums, a long finish hinting at prunes but all moderated by real freshness. Unique and appealing.

COLOMBELLE ROUGE COTES DE GASCOGNE 2007. Fruity with good acid, very deep color and a definite taste of bubble gum. Why would someone take tannat grapes and try to make Beaujolais? There is a limit to chemistry and marketing, and this, for me, is that limit. I suppose it is not objectively a bad wine, but it pissed me off.

Skouras Red 2006. An undistinguished Greek wine made mostly from cabernet grapes. Not offensive but needs more freshness and some aromatics.

Marques de Moral Valdepenas Crianza 2004. This tempranillo was fresh and pretty at first, but there was a medicinal aftertaste that, well, left a bad taste in my mouth.

Raimat Tempranillo Costers del Segre 2003. A pleasant wine with no special distinction. I found it a little hard on the finish and wonder if there is too much oak.

Agricola de Borja Borsao 2007. Traditionally one of the great values in wine (I paid $7), this was a respectable wine, lively if not complex. I'd be happy to have it, but I think the next wine knocks the socks off this one.

*Don Ramon Campo de Borja 2006. A blend of 75 percent garnacha and 25 percent tempranillo, this fruity $8 wine is ripe, spicy and complex. Put it in a lineup with some $40 Chateauneuf du Pape and it will more than hold its own.

Crucillon Campo de Borja 2005. Balanced, almost elegant, easy to enjoy but not especially exciting.

D'Aragon Garnacha 2007. A dark and perfumed wine, international in style, smooth drinking. Everyone will like this, no one will remember it.

*Red Diamond Cabernet 2006. This Washington wine is about the best bargain there is in cabernet (given the competition, maybe I should say the only bargain). It hits all the notes—black currants, tobacco, chocolate—while remaining light and fresh. It is definitely not from Napa, not rich or velvety and is meant to go to dinner, not to a tasting.

Fattoria della Vitae, Chianti Colli Senesi 2006. Just Chianti, tart, red, fruity, appetizing and a good friend to Italian food.

SANTA MARTINA TOSCANA ROSSO 2005. A more ambitious Italian—smooth, international, ambitious, "don't call me Chianti, I'm a super Tuscan." Not bad if you go for the type.

COL DES VENTS CORBIERES 2005. This is a lush, comforting southern French wine, with bright berry flavors mingled with herbal notes. Just delicious, not showy, for Sunday dinner with the family, if you're lucky.

Rich and Famous Wines v. Cheap and Tasty Ones

(April/May 2009)

Both Tuscany and the Napa Valley are beautiful places to visit and beautiful places to be fleeced by capricious wine prices. Celebrity owners seem to set whatever prices they like and rely on their names, their glamour and the gorgeous views to reconcile their customers to the cost. I've tasted too many $100 Napa cabernets and so-called Super Tuscans that were clearly inferior to Bloomington's local Creekbend cabernet from Oliver Vineyards for less than half the price.

From more rationally priced areas, and influenced by the current economic mood, I thought it would be worthwhile to identify exactly what you have a right to expect when you pay more than a basic $10 to $15 for a bottle. First, I had two sauvignon blancs from Big Red: from Chile, a 2008 Santa Ema for under $9, and from Sonoma, a 2007 J. Rochioli for four times that much. The Santa Ema was a pleasure to drink, with smooth, lingering lemony flavors. The Rochioli was obviously related: its fruity flavors were subtler and more intriguing, as a ripe cantaloupe is to lemonade, and there were hints of other flavors, maybe honey and stone.

Then I paired two sparkling wines from Sahara Mart. A Spanish Cava, made by Avinyo for $16, was grapefruity with a background of yeast and energetic little bubbles. It didn't taste much like real French Champagne but was delicious and fun in its own right. I matched it

A bottle of 2005 Pégaü, safely in Pat Baude's cellar.

with a favorite artisanal grower of Champagne, a Hébrart Brut ($52 at Sahara Mart). This was a stunning wine, with delicate flavors of lemon and lime, apples, flowers, spice and butter. The Avinyo was still good, but it seemed kind of simple by comparison, an anonymous fashion model up against Kate Winslet.

For the third match, I took two wines from Big Red, both made by Domaine du Pégaü in France's southern Rhône Valley. The first, 2006 Pegovino ($17), is a bright red wine with a lively, fresh feel and flavors of cherry with a black pepper accent. Drink it with an herb-roasted chicken and dream of June in Provence. The second, Châteauneuf du Pape Cuvée Réservée 2005 ($80), was a different matter altogether. The moment I opened it, I was surrounded by scents of flowers and berries, with no need at all to swirl and sniff. Wow! The flavor was promising too, smoke and chocolate and raspberry, but for now a little dense and tight. Put this in a cool, quiet place for a few years and it might well be as good as any wine I have ever drunk. But for dinner tonight, the Pegavino will make more friends and the difference in price will buy dinner besides.

My conclusion? If you're spending more, you're always entitled to finesse and complexity. These can be worth it for a special meal with time to talk and drink but can get lost in a quick, noisy or spicy meal. And for expensive red wines, it's easy to pay more for a wine that would have been delicious four years later. Still, I liked the Pégaü enough that I am definitely buying some lottery tickets. Wish me luck!

WINES FOR DRINKING OUTDOORS

(JUNE/JULY 2009)

You know that daydream where you're sitting outside a café by the sea in St. Tropez, trying to remember why topless bikinis are illegal in Indiana and drinking cool wine that tastes like nectar? The wine isn't as good as you think, it's just drinking it outdoors that makes it seem that way. Now's the season for taking wine outdoors, and it's worth paying attention to that ambience.

The rich oaky wines that comforted in February taste flat outside in June. But a chilly rosé will make your dandelions look like jonquils for an hour. We're in luck for rosé in Bloomington. Manolo's Wines is a Bloomington-based importer gaining a national reputation for artisanal organic wines from Spain. Manolo's 2007 Calderona, widely available here in the low teens, is a sunset-colored wine with bracing and spicy berry scents and an amazing depth of flavor—one of the world's best pink wines.

Light white wines are nice outside, but thicker whites, chardonnays for example, lack freshness. The problem has been accentuated by sniffy critics who ask for "anything but chardonnay." These people are probably the same people who say they never watch television (except PBS), claim not even to know what a Krispy Kreme is and conspicuously display Marcel Proust on their living room tables. Anyway, the problem is that sauvignon blanc, an easy and lighter alternative to California chardonnay, is now raised on steroids

Sunshine through a light white wine.

to mimic chardonnay for those who publicly disdain it. If you really don't want chardonnay, what you do want is grüner veltliner, a fragrant Austrian treat with tart, clean fruit flavors. An outstanding bargain right now, and a lovely party wine, Hugl's 2008 is a tangy example with grapefruit scents and grüner's special signature hint of ground pepper (Big Red, $11 for a full-liter bottle). I also like a Rainer Wess 2005 for its mineral purity and lively long-lasting flavors of lime and Granny Smith apples (Sahara Mart East, $23).

Red wines outdoors have a special problem. They will not refresh unless they are a little bit cool, spending maybe thirty minutes in the refrigerator on the way outside. But the red wines that would usually accompany the hamburgers or steaks of summer, cabernet especially, become excessively tannic, even gritty, when chilled. The answer is syrah—not the syrupy kind from Australia or Napa but the modern charmers from the central California coast. I think these are the most exciting new wines being made in America right now, and luckily, the market price hasn't completely caught up. I had a Baileyana from Edna Valley, a wine with earthy flavors elevated by cherry and floral notes (Sahara Mart, $20). If you try this wine, open it a couple of hours in advance to let the aroma develop. Also delicious with a slight chill, Foley's 2006 from the Santa Rita Hills delivered a smooth mixture of plum and raspberry flavors (Big Red, $23).

Despite serious efforts involving lots of zinfandel, I have failed to find any wine for the true outdoor summer meal, the mixture of pig, smoke, spice and sugar that is real southern barbecue. The best I can suggest is to follow Dolly Parton's advice in *Steel Magnolias* when she calls sweet tea "the house wine of the South."

Why Start a Wine Cellar?

(August/September 2009)

Vanity is one reason to start a wine cellar. At a dinner in Chicago last year, I was seated next to a couple way above my income class. When I later Googled them to see what they did, the only activity I found was giving money to charity in $20 million chunks. Probably I should have Googled their grandparents. As the conversation wound inevitably to their Lake Geneva house, I learned that it was so cold when they entertained in the wine cellar that guests were uncomfortable. The problem was solved by buying used mink coats at a vintage clothing store and keeping them in the cellar. Apparently the very rich, like my college fraternity brothers, enjoyed putting on ratty clothes and getting drunk in the basement.

Conspicuous consumption aside, there are good practical reasons to store some wine at home. Sometimes you find a delicious wine and it won't be there six months later—only the overpriced dogs linger in stores. And there are some wines that really do gain from being aged a few years. Right now, the 2007 wines from the southern Rhône Valley meet both tests. Fifty million gallons of red wine are grown in the Rhône, and forty million are quickly dispatched to wash down steak frites in Paris. The remainder includes some distinguished wines with rich dark fruit and solid bracing structure.

The 2007 vintage is, thanks especially to the idolized critic Robert Parker's enthusiasm, already reputed to be the best vintage not only of this short

Pat Baude's wine cellar—formerly a coat closet.

century but perhaps of all time. Exaggeration or not, the wines are without question powerful, delicious and pure.

The best examples are just arriving in Bloomington, from dozens of small producers. The easy way to find the best is to check the label for a reliable importer. I have never been disappointed (or paid too much) for wines imported by Kermit Lynch, Eric Solomon, Peter Wygant or Fran Kysela. The least expensive (in the teens) will be labeled simply "Côtes du Rhône." They are likely to be medium-bodied, tasting of blackberries or cherries and with scents of flowers or sometimes anise. These can be drunk as soon as you buy them but should stay fresh for a year or two. The big step up is to wines named after certain selected villages in the area—the best will be Gigondas, Vacqueyras or Cairanne—and priced in the twenties. Tempting now, these wines should gain greatly in complexity and smoothness if cellared for two years or so.

This kind of practical cellaring does not require expensive equipment, let alone mink coats. Perfect long-term cellaring probably needs controlled humidity and a steady temperature of fifty-five degrees. The exact conditions, however, have never been empirically validated. Even Robert Parker keeps hardier wines in the warmer part of his cellar, where the temperature reaches sixty-four degrees. Storage at the world-famous Château Margaux is sixty-six degrees, and my spare closet is currently sixty-seven degrees.

Any of these spots would be fine for 2007 Rhônes for a year or two, although they would be questionable for fragile wines like pinot or Champagne. Of course, if you're at all handy with a hammer, you could put to good use Richard Gold's trusted guidebook, *How and Why to Build a Wine Cellar* (The Wine Appreciation Guild).

Finding the Right Pinot Noir for Thanksgiving Isn't Easy

(October/November 2009)

Pinot noir and roasted turkey were made for each other. This ought to make the choice of a bottle for the Thanksgiving table a no-brainer. Of course, the traditional side dishes are wine-killers. No wine can survive cranberry relish, even though a tangy hard cider from Oliver Winery would be perfect with the bittersweet relish itself. The creamed onions call out for dark beer, and maybe some mead would be good with the candied yams. One day, a trendy chef will produce a deconstructed dégustation de merci-donnant tasting menu so each dish can have its due. Meanwhile, we have to go with the turkey.

The wine surely should be American for this holiday. Zinfandel, the essence of American wine history, is too brambly to flatter the rich meatiness of a good turkey, while cabernet sauvignon's tannins overwhelm the meat's slight sweetness. Pinot noir, on the other hand, is fresh and smooth but not biting or heavy. Its inner cool plays to the subtlety of the bird.

Still, there are two problems with American pinot at Thanksgiving. First is the identity crisis of this Old World grape in the New World. French burgundies, typically 100 percent pinot, usually strive for balance, complexity and a quality known as "earthiness." American growers often prize instead fruit and concentration. Arguments about the true nature of the variety are unbelievably heated, even by contemporary Internet standards.

Playing roulette with California pinot noirs.

The reality remains that pinot noir is like a box of chocolates: "You never know what you're gonna get." You might find, and some people are looking for, a ripe, alcoholic fruit bomb that makes an almost cocktail-like statement. This is the sort of pinot that sommeliers sell with talk of "sex in a glass." There are some luscious wines like this, especially from Sonoma's Russian River Valley—good choices for a private dinner with Scarlett Johansson but not so much for Thanksgiving with Grandma and the kids.

The second problem with pinot noir is that good examples are usually hard to find and harder to pay for. Browse the list of topflight pinots from California and Oregon and you will often find that you have to be on the wineries' direct shipping list to get any. (And direct shipping is rarely legal in Indiana.) Even then, $50 to $80 a bottle is what passes for a bargain in that market. The combination of these two problems is the reason wine lovers say, "Pinot will break your heart."

But this year, natural forces are on our side. The 2007 California vintage had a long and sunny but not hot September, producing a generous quantity of balanced wines with moderate alcohol, complex flavors and reasonable prices. Two examples, priced in the teens, are widely available in Bloomington this fall. My favorite is the MacMurray Ranch Central Coast. A beautiful purple, this wine has a dark cherry scent, flavors of the fall forest and restrained notes of smoke and vanilla from oak aging. If you like a little more excitement and a little less balance, the La Crema Sonoma Coast is an attractive choice—a floral scent and a medley of red fruit flavors. Tasting these two wines side by side would be an easy way to experience the stylistic range of California pinot without breaking the bank.

2010 Could Be a Very Good Year

(December 2009/January 2010)

The year 2010 will be a good time to buy wine. First, the 2007 vintage is still in large supply locally. In Germany, in California and in the Rhône Valley, this is the best year in about the last ten, and it's time to stock up. Prices remain in la-la land for the first growths favored by investment bankers and Russian billionaires, but economic conditions have not allowed across-the-board increases.

Second, there are special opportunities in Australia. Until last year, the big shiraz fruit bombs from the hot Barossa Valley made friends everywhere and sold easily for $30 to $50. The Australian wine industry, seemingly determined to kill the goose that laid the golden eggs, marketed ever-cheaper and coarser versions of soft sweet shiraz. At one point, an Australian brand called Yellowtail became the bestselling red wine in the United States, overpriced at well under $10. This was enough to destroy the mystique.

Not only has Yellowtail fallen to eighteenth among imports, but the cheapened image has also deflated all Australian wines. A good example from the ocean-cooled McLaren Vale is Mitolo's 2007 Jester cabernet, one of the world's real bargains ($23 at Big Red). The wine is made in part from dried grapes, which give depth and complexity to flavors of dark fruit and a touch of oak. With your next Asian dish, try any of the rieslings available

A Rias Baixas from Pat Baude's cellar.

here in the middle teens. Mark Twain wrote, "Wagner's music is better than it sounds." These bottles show that Australian wine is better than it tastes.

The third bit of news, a silver lining I guess, is that the economic crisis has helped the wine market to loosen patterns that were at risk of becoming permanently boring. With lots of money chasing calibrated status symbols, the corporate wine world was beginning to look like General Motors: Chilean merlot for the Chevy, chardonnay for the Buick and Napa cabernet for the Escalade. But as people look for bargains, they are discovering not only lower prices but also satisfying experiences.

This is not the time to look for poorer versions of what we used to drink (or drive, or wear, or do). It's time to look for different things whose prices have not yet been inflated by mass demand. In white wine, for example, try a Spanish wine from Rias Baixas, made from the albariño grape. Burgans ($12 at Big Red) or Nora ($15 at Sahara Mart) are crisp, elegant wines with a light body, scents of spring and flavors of melon and something like marmalade. They are also on the list in local restaurants for a reasonable toll.

For red wine, take malbec from Argentina seriously for a change. Basic and good $10 malbecs have been around for a few years, but now we are beginning to see, for about twice that much, beautiful wines that make no compromises. BenMarco 2007 ($19 at Sahara Mart) has exuberant flavors of cherry and raspberry, balanced by satisfying forest flavors. Kaiken Ultra 2006 ($21 at Big Red) has more subdued fruit with a bouquet of violets and spices. Even if the economy comes back, I wouldn't replace these wines with Bordeaux just because I could. Instead, I'll be saving up for some 2008 Oregon pinots.

When to Send that Bottle Back

(February/March 2010)

I was in an expensive Detroit restaurant near a man with an expensive suit who was ordering expensive wine in a loud voice. Somehow I knew, and so did the sommelier if I read his body language right, that the wine would be rejected when it got to his table. I didn't feel sorry for the management when this happened since its selling price for the first bottle would have been fair for two of them in the first place. I did feel sorry for the woman at the table. Her body language made it clear she didn't want another bottle of Chateau Lafite-Rothschild at all. What she seemed to want was another pink cosmopolitan and a different companion.

Yes, there are decisions to be made after an eager waiter has passed the wine list and given us an appraising look. Faced with a challenging or unfamiliar list, it's easy to feel insecure and vulnerable to the implicit pressure of overspending. In a good, formal urban restaurant, there will be a professionally trained sommelier. His profession is to help you find a wine you can afford and enjoy. If you're embarrassed to talk money, there is a code. Point to a wine with a price you choose and ask for "something along this line." Where there is no sommelier, the server should have been taught to make suggestions—usually sound but rarely exciting. If you want exciting, the best bet is to get hold of the wine list in advance or ask around before you go.

William Baude, recoiling from a bad glass.

In Bloomington, it is easy to find an acceptable bottle in the town's good restaurants. But exciting bottles are there too. Just in the last month, I have had several special wines. Looking, for example, at whites priced in the thirties, I had two beauties. The Nora Rias Baixas at Restaurant Tallent is a fresh Spanish wine with notes of lemon and melon—a perfect match for the oysters on the half shell. And the Tablas Creek Côtes de Blanc at Finch's Brasserie is proof that Paso Robles is becoming one of California's great sites for Rhône-style wines.

The second decision is when the wine comes and an ounce is splashed in the host's glass—or, worse, the host is interviewing you for a job and passes the glass expectantly to you for the ritual taste. The thing to remember that makes it easy is this: you are not judging the wine overall, looking for the aroma of macerated quince. You are looking for obvious faults, and there are really only four, each with a telltale sign. If the glass smells like wet cardboard, the wine is "corked." If it tastes or smells like rancid almonds, it's oxidized and is only good for making vinegar. If it smells like an active barnyard, it's been infected with "brett." And if it smells like sulfur, it is "reduced." In all these cases, the wine goes back, no questions asked.

If you just don't like the bottle because you wanted smoky slate and it has tropical fruit, tough luck. You probably should have taken the waiter's advice. Usually, however, if you say nicely that the wine is fine and you'll pay for it but would like to order a different one, the house will graciously take it off the bill. If so, remember to tip handsomely, tell your friends and go back.

Spring Is Time to Try a New Grape

(April/May 2010)

About three hundred varieties of wine grapes grow around the world. A wine drinker who has tasted one hundred can apply for membership online in the Wine Century Club. There are no particular privileges of membership. This is a case where the journey, not the destination, is the thing.

A wine drinker who follows the path of least resistance probably drinks fewer than a dozen varietals in a year—cabernet, pinot noir, merlot, syrah, chardonnay, sauvignon blanc, riesling, grenache, zinfandel and maybe a fling with pinot grigio. Adding to the potential for monotony, many of these wines are made in the same "international style," fruit-forward, oaky and alcoholic.

Spring is a good time to play around, and I can think of three temptations easily available here. Zweigelt is young by wine-grape standards, first produced in Austria during the 1920s. It can survive in otherwise inhospitably cool zones. In the current climate, there are even tiny plantings in Belgium and England. The wine is fresh and floral. Big Red has Hugl Zweigelt from Austria for $12 a liter. Drink it with a light chill and enjoy violet fragrances, a taste of sour cherries and hints of spice. Sahara Mart has a more complex Austrian version by Umathum in the low $20s—blueberry as much as black cherry, with herbal and mineral notes and a teasing, bitter finish. Tradition pairs these wines with wienerschnitzel, but any light meal or picnic works.

These are several different varieties of grapes, although not the zweigelt, mencia or chambourcin.

It is almost impossible to tell most grapes apart by the grapes themselves, though some experts can differentiate them by the leaves. These are pinot noir.

Chardonnay grapes.

Cabernet sauvignon grapes.

Another happy diversion would be the mencia grape, grown mainly in the Bierzo region of northwest Spain. The mencia grape, until twenty years ago, was dismissed as simply a Spanish clone of the French cabernet franc grape, itself usually brushed off as "not serious"—meaning it made cheerful wine for happy Frenchmen rather than the sort of expensive juice connoisseurs sniff with each other. DNA tests now show that mencia has nothing to do with cabernet franc. It turns out that good wine from Bierzo hillsides is one of today's rare bargains. There are two good examples at Sahara Mart, both priced in the mid-teens. Pucho Bierzo is electric purple, smells of blackberries and anise and delivers flavors hinting at chocolate cherries, a little like pinot noir with zip. Baltos Bierzo is similar, a bit brighter and less complex, with a note of something like cranberries. Either wine would be perfect with chicken and tomatoes.

A third choice is closer to home. Oliver Winery makes a lively dry rosé from chambourcin grapes. Chambourcin is a French hybrid used for mediocre wine in the Loire Valley but showing promise in the eastern United States. Oliver's rosé, from grapes grown locally, has fresh berry flavors with good underlying substance. As the weather warms, this should be first choice for locavores. Butler Winery's semidry version of chambourcin rosé, also made from Monroe County grapes, won a double gold medal at the 2009 Indiana State Fair.

If you really want to rack up esoteric varietals, though, you need to travel. During a couple of months lecturing in the former Soviet Union, I got to taste the likes of tsimlyansky, saperavi and plavai. Mikhail Gorbachev ripped them up to discourage alcoholism. In my opinion, he would have discouraged drinking even more if he'd increased the plantings.

When Buying "Organic," Be Wary of Wine Labels

(June/July 2010)

Pure natural wine is a good thing, and finding it should be as easy as reading a label. But every wine buyer knows the frustration of actually decoding a label. Regulation of alcoholic drinks, like regulation of Wall Street investment banks, is not transparent and not designed with the consumer foremost. So we end up in the wine store, puzzling through words like "organic," "sustainable" and "biodynamic."

To begin with, be leery of bottles called "organic wine." These words are regulated by federal law and certify not only that the grapes were grown without industrial chemicals but also that the wine was made without added sulfur and has a low sulfite content. (Sulfites are widespread and deadly for a small number of people, who should be under an allergist's care, but not a health concern for the rest of us.) The problem is that sulfites are necessary to prevent wine from spoiling, and "organic wine" is at high risk of contamination.

Instead, look for the description "made from organic grapes." These wines have naturally grown fruit but can be bottled with a little sulfur dioxide to keep them fresh. The term is legally restricted to grapes meeting federal legal requirements, but foreign producers are eligible if they meet the standards. Some international producers do comply. Jean Bousquet, for example, is a Frenchman who makes wine from certified organic malbec

A "biodynamic" wine. For a less mystical guarantee of natural wine, look for wine "made from organic grapes."

grapes in Argentina with the North American market in mind. The result is spicy with dark berry flavors but, like many naturally made wines, balanced and not bristling with alcohol (Sahara Mart, $13).

Smaller foreign producers may find it too burdensome to certify their organic grapes specifically for the American market and, even though they are certified as organic by the European Union, are not allowed the actual word "organic" on a label in this country. This restriction particularly affects some artisanal growers making beautiful low-cost wines in small quantities. There are two fine examples from J.M. Lafage, who has several vineyards scattered around southwest France and northern Spain. His Grenache Noir (Big Red, $14) has delicious red berry flavors with a clean mineral base. Côté d'Est (Big Red, $12), a white wine made from chardonnay along with traditional southern French varieties, exuberantly mixes citrus, flowers and bright spices in what has to be the single best buy in town.

Be aware, of course, that European farmers are as greedy as anybody else and some look for quick profits from harsh chemicals. In Champagne, for instance, commercial vineyards are often fertilized with municipal solid waste collected on the streets of Paris.

By now most of the world seems to be hooked on *Avatar* and needs no urging to seek health and joy in connecting with nature. Me, I'm convinced by a story from Bobby Wallace, Big Red's corporate wine director. He was at Ehler Vineyards, a Napa biodynamic estate—"biodynamic" combines organic, homeopathic, spiritual and even astrological practices. Jogging by Ehler in the morning, he was struck by the fullness of life in the vineyards, by the birds, the buzzing insects, the rustling of small animals and the diversity of trees and plants. Biodynamic theory may be mystical and beyond scientific validation. Even so, when Wallace told me of other vineyards he passed, where the workers were using hazmat suits to treat the silent vines, I started thinking well of mysticism.

If You Must: What Wines to Buy in the Supermarket

(August/September 2010)

When my son was six, we'd all slipped away for a short vacation. When we got there, Jonathan became increasingly agitated as he carefully checked out the situation, peering into the empty refrigerator, opening doors and climbing around. I thought at first he was missing the new puppy we'd left at home. Finally I got it—he was afraid of hunger—when he beamed, pulled me over to the telephone and said, "It's okay, Dad, there will be pizza!" When I repeated that story to him years later, he replied that I was exactly the same. On vacation, at the first trip to the grocery in the nearest lakeside town, I disappeared anxiously for twenty minutes, reappearing with a couple of bottles of decent wine and obvious relief.

Looking for good wine in a grocery store is perfectly logical, which is no doubt why 40 percent of the country's wine is sold in supermarkets. After you settle on the salmon or the ribs, then you know what you want to drink. In this state, however, you'd better not pick the bratwurst for dinner; it's a crime to buy cold beer in an Indiana grocery store. Even so, we may be luckier than residents of the fifteen states where it's illegal to buy wine with your groceries at all, although as compensation in most of those states you can pick up a chilled six-pack. All this is supposed to keep children safe, but I forget how.

Still, finding good wine in a supermarket is not easy. Most big chains centralize their purchasing, which means they mainly buy food and drink

You can buy pretty good wine at a chain grocery store, if you know what to look for.

in industrial quantities from giant corporations. This seems to work well for high-fructose corn drinks like colas, but it's the enemy of wine with character. Of course, small local grocery stores are a different matter. Bloomingfoods and Sahara Mart are stocked with distinctive wines that don't come from the vinous equivalent of British Petroleum.

When necessary, I count on two brands available in lots of stores, here and nationally. Chateau Ste. Michelle makes wine in Seattle from grapes grown across the mountains in eastern Washington. A good wine store will carry its expensive single-vineyard wines but also make straightforward varietal wines selling widely for around $12. The cabernet sauvignon is an amazing value—gorgeous purple wine, medium-bodied, with fresh cherry scents and easygoing fruit flavors. The riesling radiates melon and pear scents, with flavors of citrus and an appetizing touch of honey. It's not bone-dry and so makes a good companion for a spicy Asian stir-fry.

The other choice is Bogle, a California producer whose $10 wines come from the Sacramento Valley, far from Napa's grossly inflated real estate. Its petite sirah is an unusual and interesting wine. That grape, related to syrah but not the same in spelling or flavor, makes sharp acid wine in Europe, but this Californian is full-bodied and peppery, with flavors and scents of dark fruit. Bogle's zinfandel is a similar full-throated American wine, rich and fruity without being thick or cloying. The cabernet is a good wine but not so much an original. I find Bogle's white wines more ordinary. And the petite sirah, by the way, will take care of those brats when you can't get the cold beer.

Manolo: A Name to Know in Bloomington

(October/November 2010)

Some wine lovers like to talk about the bottle that changed their lives, usually something rare and expensive—Yquem, Lafite, Romanée-Conti, Screaming Eagle. For me it was Gallo Hearty Burgundy, an honest wine that, at $1.29 a bottle, made the difference between getting by and having a civilized life as an assistant professor. In those days, good honest wine was hard to find. The French wine industry seemed to proceed on the assumption that gullible Americans should be grateful to part with their hard currency for anything at all made by a man with a beret. The rest of Europe hardly bothered to export, and California kept its best at home.

All this changed thirty years ago, thanks to a handful of importers who sought out individual growers, picked wines by taste rather than by label, insisted on high standards in winemaking and financed refrigerated transportation. Names like Kermit Lynch and Joe Dressner have become guarantees to American buyers that imported wine can be pure, honest and interesting. There is now a name in Bloomington to add to this list of sources for authentic imported wine. "Manolo's Wines" are imported by Manuel Hernandez-Martin, who specializes in organically made wines from small Spanish vineyards.

Manolo came to the United States thirty years ago, first to work at the University of California Medical School and then as a research scientist

The honest Gallo Hearty Burgundy, still available today.

at Indiana University. Five years ago, he gave in to his real ambition and started an importing firm with one pallet of wine. Now he imports fifty to seventy-five times that much, mainly to sell throughout Indiana but also with growing distribution in New York, Michigan, Georgia and Tennessee. He travels the byways of Spain twice a year, visiting family vineyards and small cooperatives, tasting thousands of wines. It gives me hope to realize that this has become his day job.

Major Spanish producers and large cooperatives have become well known in this country and England as dependable sources of cheap and predictable wine. But Manolo is aiming to show the integrity and variety of the country's wine—Spain, in fact, has more vineyard area in cultivation than any other nation. Some of the wines will seem familiar to any contemporary drinker. The Calderona rose, for example, widely available for about $10, smells like fresh berries with elegant long-finishing flavor. The respected critic Stephen Tanzer, not known for easy praise, called the 2006 vintage "one of the liveliest, most delicious rosados I tasted." Or El Molino de Puelles, priced in the upper twenties, is a classic example of the Rioja, Spain's best-known wine region—a smooth red with spicy dark fruit, silky texture and subtle oak flavors of coffee and vanilla.

The portfolio also offers wines that might be less familiar. Miudiño, for example, is made from albariño grapes. Ordinary albariños are tart and clean but often not much more; this one also brings in pears, apples and maybe cantaloupe and is a delight to drink before dinner. Damana 5 is a bright red wine with scents of flowers and tastes of cherry plus tantalizing bass chords of something darker. These two wines are priced in the middle teens. Accompanied by the rose, they would be a generous welcome for open-minded Thanksgiving guests.

Books About Wine Make Nice Gifts

(December 2010/January 2011)

One benefit of having a reputation as a wine lover is that you almost never get a necktie for Christmas. Still, we all have friends who simply refuse to believe that one can never have too much wine. These friends should at least be thinking of books about wine, which have the added benefit that they can be sent through the United States mail without sharing the proceeds with a mandatory state-licensed wholesaler.

There are two well-known favorites for those lucky enough not to have read them already. Don and Petie Kladstrup's 2001 *Wine & War* (Broadway Books) tells the inside story of French wine under Nazi occupation. Allied intelligence, for example, had advance notice of Rommel's campaign in Egypt because French producers secretly reported the destinations to which the Nazis shipped Champagne in anticipatory celebration. And Chateau Margaux successfully hid a Jewish family for most of the war.

Many of the exploits of the French resistance centered on the Burgundy house of Joseph Drouhin. Someone could be very happy to get a gift of the Kladstrups' book and a bottle of one of Drouhin's wines from Sahara Mart.

Kermit Lynch, one of the visionary wine importers who changed the scene for Americans, tells how that happened in his 1988 book, *Adventures on the Wine Route* (North Point Press). Give a friend this book and a bottle of wine imported by Lynch—and watch, you'll see.

A small sampling of Pat Baude's wine library.

American wine has some tales too. The Norton grape, for example, first developed in Virginia during Thomas Jefferson's lifetime, was the most planted wine grape in the eastern United States back when Missouri was what Napa is now. In 1873, at a famous tasting in Vienna, the Missouri Norton was judged one of the world's great wines. It almost completely disappeared by the 1920s and is now showing up in small quantities in Virginia and the Midwest. Todd Kliman's 2010 book, *The Wild Vine* (Clarkson Potter), recounts this story, which should charm anyone interested in wines from eastern America, especially if it is accompanied by a bottle of actual Norton from a visit to the French Lick Winery.

So far as American history itself goes, the big drinking story is of course Prohibition. Daniel Okrent's *Last Call: The Rise and Fall of Prohibition* (Scribner) is a readable explanation that Prohibition was about feminism, religion, labor, immigration and taxation as much as alcohol. It should be required reading for any serious drinker, except that it is so readable that there's no reason to require it. Pair it with a bottle of Indiana's one artisanal gin, fittingly called Prohibition Gin, from Heartland Distillers.

And there are two new books exploring contemporary controversies in the world of wine appreciation. Matt Kramer, the gold standard for wine columnists, has a new collection of essays, *Matt Kramer on Wine* (Sterling Epicure). His work always shows, in his own words, that "wine writing can be more than a string of fruit-and-flower taste descriptors culminating in a slam-bam-thank-you-ma'am score." And Terry Theise, a wine importer so charmingly erudite that his catalogues are sometimes resold after they expire, has published a spiritual inquiry into wine's mystical power, *Reading Between the Wines* (University of California Press). Maybe you'll love it. Maybe you will react as he reports one reader did to a catalogue: this is "pretentious new-age bullshit." But reading it with one of Theise's imported Mosels might enhance the life force.

A Time to Buy

(February/March 2011)

This spring is probably the best time to buy wine in my memory. Each of the last three years has produced some very good and remarkably different wines. In 2007, California cabernet sauvignons showed an unusual richness and relaxed thoroughness. The 2008 Oregon pinot noirs were as dark and romantic as the best pinots. The Beaujolais of 2009 gave the penetrating aroma of fresh, free wine.

All too often California cabernets are headstrong, too spicy and short of freshness. The remarkable thing about the 2007s, however, is that there are at least three inexpensive wines that hit serious highs of flavor. California cabernets of this quality often cost several hundred dollars. These 2007 cabernets show complexity, seriousness and flavor that lasts for minutes. First, a favorite for more than a century, the Louis Martini Cabernet Sauvignon shows a beautiful color of blackberries and deep scents of smoky soil. The taste is full and round without being pushy or loud. Second is the Robert Mondavi Napa Cabernet Sauvignon. The rich and silky texture of this purple wine adds savory and aromatic herbal deep notes. The color alone will draw you into the picture. The third is perhaps the most interesting. Beaulieu Cabernet Sauvignon Rutherford has the deep color of a true cabernet marked with fine touches of spice and exotic tea.

A few of the bottles in Pat Baude's cellar (with a cautionary note written by William).

The best of the 2008 Oregon pinot noirs display vibrant and spicy color. Three reasonably priced pinots demonstrate intense flavors mixing cinnamon, cranberry and black cherry. Even more impressive, the Ponzi Pinot Noir has an aromatic black flavor with a powerful crush of black fruit. The A to Z Wineworks Pinot Noir is an inexpensive but fully ready-to-drink wine. It has a bright flavor of dried roses, cherry skins and bitter peppers. Finally, the Domaine Drouhin Oregon Pinot Noir Laurene Dundee Hills tastes of strawberries and red flowers, but unfortunately, it will probably not be ready to drink for another ten years.

People often dismiss Beaujolais wine as simple, satisfying and balanced. Once every ten or twenty years, though, the wine becomes rich and irresistible. The 2009s are probably the richest Beaujolais wines ever made. At this moment, it is too early to predict how these wines will turn out. The one thing that is sure is that these wines will exhibit extreme fruit, pure color and something startling. My guess is that a dozen different Beaujolais will have a dozen different tastes.

Remarkably, most of these wines are all ready to drink now. But putting them aside for another five years would give them depth. In any case, this is definitely the time to put some serious wine away. Keeping it will be the hard part.

Everyday Life with Wine

I had planned to write a little meditation on the importance of everyday wine. Recently, I've had a delicious South African Sauvignon Blanc from Jardin and a quite different Sauvignon de Saint Bris from Verget, more famous for his good value chardonnay. These were both priced in the teens, both racy and fun to drink (I'll buy the Jardin again, probably not the Verget, which is a little more expensive). My theme was to be a defense of mediocrity. I don't especially like beer, so I have no trouble at all saying that I would rather have Chimay once a month than Bud every day. Wine fans like to advise one to drink good wine once a week rather than ordinary wine every day. Not me. I love wine. Give me honest clean wine every day. I love my friends. I'd have dinner with my friends every day rather than saving up for a banquet with John Roberts. (Julia Roberts is in a different category, for obvious reasons.)

So I went to Lexis to find a celebrated example of the "life is too short to drink mediocre wine" quotation often attributed to Lady Pamela Harlech, second wife of the British ambassador to John Kennedy's court. As I recall, she served Barbaresco and Montrachet at cocktail parties. But the successive tragedies of the Harlech family took the wind out of my sails. Lord Harlech died in a traffic accident, as had his father. His older brother, who would otherwise have inherited the title, shot himself. His sister, who

Pat Baude's wine cellar, which provided "honest clean wine every day."

was once engaged to Eric Clapton, died impoverished and of an alcohol-drug interaction in a London bedsit. Lady Pamela herself was banned from driving because of alcohol-related charges. The eight-thousand-acre estate had to be sold to pay the death duties, which I shall now think of as a Barbaresco tax. Perhaps the ultimate indignity, the *Express* wrote thus of the sixth Baron Harlech, facing drunk driving charges himself four years ago: "The small, dark figure in the dock of Dolgellau magistrates court in North Wales was a sorry sight. With his lambchop sideburns and his jetblack hair greased back behind his ears, he looked like a cross between Fred West and a reject from the Seventies band Showaddywaddy." Myself, I have a $15 Vouvray, 2002 Chateau Gaudrelle, chilling for tomorrow night. Life is too long to drink great wine all the time, thank heaven.

Addendum

I ended my last post looking forward to a 2002 Chateau Gaudrelle, using it as an example of an ordinary wine that could still give a lot of pleasure. What a stupid thing to write! There was nothing even remotely ordinary about this elegant and steely Vouvray, with lively fruit and rich mineral flavors. I have spent some of the intervening time educating myself about this and other wines of the Loire Valley. I was helped by a few days at the beach on Lake Michigan, which I began by taking advantage of a special offer from Sam's in Chicago. Sam's had assembled fifteen pretty much unknown (to me and most Americans anyway) Loire wines through the services of Tom Calder, a specialized broker in Paris. This was not an expensive venture, at $250 for the fifteen. It has been, in fact, a pretty cheap lesson in the great pleasures of the world of honest wine.

The Loire is about as far north as any wine I'd care to drink can be made (excluding, thus, the entire wine production of the United Kingdom—grape, parsnip or rhubarb). This far north, in a chilly year, the vintage can be so acid it hurts, but in a warm year, the results can be lively and stimulating. Luckily, both 2002 and 2003 were warm to heat-wave hot, and the wines are just wonderful. There are two good examples, both white wines from Chenin Blanc grapes, each less than $15, available at Big Red—the Chateau Gaudrelle Vouvray and an Aubert la Chapelle Coteaux du Loir (not a misprint; the Loir, masculine, is a tributary of the Loire, feminine) 2003. The Chapelle comes close to what apple cider would be if it really tasted like fresh tart apples. It was perfect with shrimp cooked with chipotles. The

Gaudrelle is a touch richer and could accompany a roast chicken. Either would be just the right thing for a young goat cheese. I recently got my copy of *Mondovino* from Netflix. This documentary is the controversial indictment of the wine world's global infatuation with rich, overripe, overpriced and too-similar wines allegedly manipulated to please Robert Parker and his hedonistic, supposedly sheep-like followers. I shall have several Loires on hand as antidotes to this trend.

Sahara Champagne

If Mercedes Benz made Champagne, I'd want to drink the BMW. Mercedes used to make exciting cars. Once they were established as the world's best, it then turned to hanging onto that reputation by making cars that reassure the owner of his worth rather than exciting him. The big-brand Champagne houses must have a similar marketing plan. Having spent fortunes on advertising and good solid winemaking over the years, their labels reassure the purchaser that he must indeed be a person with good taste and spare change. The reassurance is nice, of course. If your girlfriend picks you up in a Mercedes with a bottle of Moet et Chandon Champagne, you have a lot to look forward to. To achieve this stable luxury, the big brands buy Champagne from hundreds of farmers and blend the wines of different years over time. The wine tastes the same; you can relax. A little sweet, no surprises, nothing exaggerated.

But in recent years, some individual farmers in Champagne have begun to bypass the highly advertised conglomerate-owned brands—all the brands you see advertised in the *New Yorker*—in favor of selling their own wines, unblended and made with a minimum of manipulation. These are wines that taste different from one batch to the next, wines designed to thrill you with racy flavors and vibrant textures, wines that do not speak with the polite hush of a gentleman's club. But also wines you might not like and that will not simply invoke expensive comforts. Less than 3 percent of the total crop is sold in this way as artisanal Champagne, often called "farmer fizz" or, with slightly more formality, "grower Champagne." Basic big-brand Champagne sells for $30 to $40, and the grower wines are usually $10 to $20 more. This step up to farmer fizz is the biggest bang you can get in the wine market for $10 or $20. All the famous brands also make very expensive bottles as well, typically selling for $100 or $200. These pricey bottles can be first-rate and individualistic too, of course. For myself, though, the price is simply too much, given the thrills available from good grower Champagnes. (Except maybe Krug, the one important Champagne house that makes only the best and most expensive—if Mumm is a Mercedes, Krug is the Bentley.)

The importer Terry Theise has made it his life's work to bring farmer fizz to the United States, and Sahara Mart has newly found a spot in his distribution chain. In February, Sahara Mart and Farm Restaurant held a tasting for nine different examples of these wines, and the wines are, in general, available at the Mart. I had three favorites. These three were also the least expensive (never happened that way to me before):

1) Margaine, Cuvee Traditionelle, Brut Nonvintage, $48. Champagne can be made from a mixture of grapes, pinot noir and chardonnay typically predominating. This one is 90 percent chardonnay, with a bouquet of delicate flowers, maybe honeysuckle, and fruity flavors somewhat like peach. The result is very pleasant with food—something fresh and bright, like melon with prosciutto.
2) Hebrart, Selection, Brut Nonvintage, $52. This is a little tangier than the Margaine. There are flowers in the bouquet but also a more serious note, spices perhaps. The taste definitely evokes lemons, and the whole would be a lively aperitif or good company for some smoked salmon.
3) Aubry, Brut Nonvintage, $47. This is a big boy, unusual in that a full 50 percent is neither pinot noir nor chardonnay but a red grape called pinot meunier. The result is richer than the first two, with flavors less of fruit and more of something like bread and butter. This actually tastes wonderful with popcorn, but don't tell the luxury police, who will bust you for not using caviar. I'm sure caviar would be swell.

Rum

I made a rum sidecar last night. It was very successful and nostalgic for me. My father drank Scotch with me when I came home and kept Jack Daniels for my mother's best friend. But home alone, the only spirit he drank was rum. And when I was in Paris in the 1950s, cafés smelled of rum. Cognac and whiskey were too expensive for every day in bars, but rum came from the remnants of the French empire and had big tax breaks.

I find a sidecar close to too sweet, even when I make it in the English way—two parts brandy, one part cointreau, one part lemon juice. But the added flavor of the rum gives just a little more bite. I hadn't thought about how this is really like a margarita—I make mine two parts tequila, one part liqueur, one part lime juice, and the tequila flavor is so potent it seems much more alcoholic than a Cognac sidecar. I think I might try a bourbon version—I guess the difference with a whiskey sour would just be sweetening with liqueur rather than syrup. Or maybe I will stick to rum.

Diesel Fumes

A friend gave me a glass of white wine to taste on Saturday. He hid the bottle from me, knowing that if I had seen the screwcap I would have said "Australian" and my prejudices would have engaged—"another blowsy, heavy over-manipulated bottle," I would have thought. In fact, this Australian riesling, Radford Dale 2004, was a beautiful wine. Zind Humbrecht riesling from Alsace was my first thought, except the circumstances weren't right for a $50 bottle and my Zind Humbrechts don't really taste good until I've cellared them for at least five years. (This Radford Dale is available for $18 at Big Red but not in large supply.) It's a riesling with real class, a bright gold color, a clean but bitter flavor and hints of lemon and grapefruit, as well as that special minerally note that riesling lovers unappetizingly call "diesel." I can only say that if my old MB 240D had smelled like this, I'd have it still.

Beaujolais Nouveau

November 17 at midnight (the third Thursday in November) marks the official release of Beaujolais nouveau. This is the wine made this fall from the summer's grapes. In fact, ten thousand cases have already been shipped to Japan alone, ready for celebration at the exact hour of release. The nouveau is light, fruity, pretty insubstantial and quite pleasant to drink with a little chill on it. Its international reputation is mainly a matter of marketing hype, and I, like many Beaujolais fans, used to be irritated by the hoopla. Beaujolais can be a wine of real substance too, and this flashy nouveau business tends to obscure even more the serious merits of the good stuff. By now, though, I recognize my attitude as just another form of wine crankiness. Anything that celebrates simple, honest wine is a good thing for wine's contribution to joy, for evidence, as Benjamin Franklin put it, that "God loves us, and loves to see us happy." All it takes to complete the picture is equally simple and direct food.

And here's the simple dish that's on my mind this month—a clever way to strip roast chicken to its delicious basics, thanks to the newest *Cook's Illustrated* television series with book. Heat the oven to 500 degrees Fahrenheit. (Yeah, we know that's the best way to roast a chicken, but doesn't the smoke drive you out of the kitchen? Hang on.) Cut out the backbone, easy with poultry shears but a slight nuisance with a knife, and flatten the chicken a little by smashing down on the breastbone. (This way, the thighs and the breast will be done at the same time.) Now peel and slice two russet potatoes. (They will absorb the chicken fat as it renders, which is why your kitchen won't be engulfed in acrid smoke.) Finally, and this is the genius part, get out the broiler pan, line it with foil, put the potatoes in the bottom and then put on the ridged part, with the chicken on its back on top. (This keeps the potatoes moist and the chicken greaseless.) Salt, roast for about forty-five minutes for a three-and-a-half-pound bird and you are done. The fat should pour right off the potatoes, but you can also blot them a little with a paper towel. You could also work an ounce or two of butter under the skin before you roast it. No need to brine the chicken, especially if you start with a good one; I prefer either a Maverick Farm roaster from O'Malia's or a Bell and Evans from Kroger. A simple dish that will show your nouveau at its best but wouldn't let down your expensive pinot either.

Playing With My Wine

Infusion

An Indiana thunderstorm the other night brought down several branches from our walnut trees. There were some nicely formed green walnuts on them, and I wondered if those walnuts had to be the nuisance they usually become when ripe, making it dangerous to walk outside without a helmet (these are tall old trees!) and making our footing treacherous when they lie rotting all over in the fall. Italians make a liqueur from green walnuts steeped in spirits, gathered on San Giovanni's day (June 24) and ready by Easter. The French make "vin de noix" by steeping the quartered green walnuts in red wine with sugar and brandy. The walnuts in France are supposed to be gathered after St. Jean's day (June 24, doh) but before Bastille Day, so get cracking! In the countryside, the resulting wine is sometimes served to guests, as would be the port it resembles—remember that the French, who are otherwise gods about everything they put in their stomachs, are children about their aperitifs, seeking constant sweetness, so porto, like vin de noix, is an aperitif. It is, however, an aperitif for which enormous health claims can be made. As we Americans would say, combining the antioxidants and polyphenols in red wine with those in nuts is a real power drink. I found a basic recipe in Mireille Johnson's *Cuisine of the Rose: Classical French Cooking from*

Burgundy and Lyonnais. Yesterday I put up a couple of quarts as an experiment. Drop by in January and have a taste; we'll see if this is an experiment worth repeating.

To steep the walnuts, I used a wine from Big Red, a new wine from La Vielle Ferme, called V.F. This is a 2002 Costieres de Nimes, a rich and rustic wine that is an utter steal for $5.99. Not sophisticated but a deep and rewarding product of the Perrin family, who do also make some of the most sophisticated wines of the Rhône Valley for forty times the price. Meanwhile, I also found a different recipe for vin de noix, using walnut leaves rather than the nuts, and plan to try some of that too. The leaf-based wine is supposed to be ready in October. But if you stop by in the fall, remember the helmet.

BITTER HARVEST

At the beginning of the summer, I wrote about making some vin de noix by steeping green walnuts (from my yard) in red wine with a little brandy and some simple syrup. It was bottling time over the weekend, and I have to say this is not an experiment I am likely to repeat. The mahogany-colored result was beautiful to look at but undrinkably bitter. Maybe the nuts were too ripe, not ripe enough, the wrong kind? With the help of an experienced wine-nutter, maybe it's worth trying again. At the same time, I also made a batch by steeping California walnut leaves (marketed for this very purpose) in the same way. I didn't have to spit this version out, but it, too, was quite bitter. I'll give it a rest and try a glass later. I was expecting something soothingly countrified and gentler, but maybe, just maybe, if I aproach it as an urbanite-kicking Campari, Dubonnet or some quinine-infused aperitif, it might work. On the success side, however, I also put up some local sour cherries in sweetened vodka and some wild blackberries in cheap Spanish brandy; both are delicious and well worth doing.

Yquem

I don't know about my favorite wine, but the one I've been obsessed with lately is Chateau d'Yquem. This was the last bottle of wine I shared with my father, sometime about 1980. I was thus tempted by the 2001, despite a price tag around $500 a bottle, as it is a serious contender for the greatest ever. I was only egged on by another, lesser but still marvelous, 2001 Sauternes, the Chateau Myrat from Big Red for about $25 for a half bottle. I shared it with a friend who thought he didn't like sweet wine and said he would just have a taste. Ha! A man of refined manners he is, but that didn't stop him from actually licking the glass (his second) when he thought I wasn't looking.

One problem with the 2001 Yquem is that it may not be drinking prime until about 2050—when I doubt that I will be. One of the surprises of the wine I had with Dad was this: a 1967, it had been badly scorched in a fire, the cork pushed out half an inch and the wine turned from lemon-colored to caramel. So we drank it on an impulse, expecting nothing, when it was a dozen years old. The heat had aged it prematurely, bringing it close to perfection. Anyway, this memory sent me looking for some older Yquem after the 2001s were released this past September. The result was that I recently spent my birthday at a Hart Davis Hart wine auction in Chicago, where I did buy some bargains and, not in the bargain category, a few half bottles of the 1990 Yquem, another revered vintage—and one that is

A 1989 Chateau d'Yquem from Pat Baude's cellar.

perhaps ready to drink now and, indeed, probably needs to be all drunk up by 2065 or so. I am a little afraid to share a bottle with any of my own children, however, in light of the family history. On the other hand, this was the very last bottle from my father's cellar, so perhaps always having one undrunk is the key. In any case, if the final act opens with Yquem, it'll sure beat Two-Buck Chuck.

Rethinking Australians

(September 2006)

Len Evans died a few weeks ago. He was a kick-ass champion of Australian wines and other Rabelaisian pursuits. People say he would come up to them, estimate their fitness and thus their longevity and say something like, "You have fourteen years to go, that's only 5,100 bottles of wine; you have no time to waste on bad wine." The end of his wine-drinking days turned my thoughts to Australian wines. Years ago, when I did more traveling in food-forsaken parts of the country, I discovered that I could almost always be happier in an Outback Steakhouse than in its Texas-style competitor, not because the meat was any better and certainly not because my cardiologist endorsed the "bloomin' onion" but only because the cheap industrial Australian wine they sold was way better than the cheap industrial-quality American wine at their competitors. In those days, even the better Australian wines, as it seemed to me, were similarly meant for grilled rich red meat in an uncomplicated, hearty way. I heard from time to time from friends who had been to Australia that there was also a world of variety in Australian wines, but I found little evidence where I shopped.

More recently, an importer called the Grateful Palate has begun to bring in some of these other wines, typically from smaller producers, often with older vines and invariably with lower yields resulting from less irrigation. Some of them are just arriving at Big Red, and I am wowed. One of them is Trevor Jones Virgin Chardonnay 2004 ($20), which also benefits from the fact that 2004 may have been the best year in South Australia for a long time. This is a chardonnay that spends zero time in oak, so it has no butterscotch or coconut. It just tastes like late summer—cantaloupe and peaches, maybe, with a squirt of citrus. It's a perfect match for fresh corn, no easy task.

And then for $32, there's a real eye-opener from Teusner, a 2005 Joshua, which is also an unoaked wine, this time red, from the classic Chateauneuf du Pape blend of grenache, mourvedre (they call it mataro) and syrah (they call it shiraz). But this tastes nothing at all like its French counterparts. A beautifully deep red, it tastes of black cherries and spicy herbs, rich but juicy, with a fresh tartness I haven't previously met in Australian wines. The other day I had it with some beef from the grill, the usual use of an Australian red for me. The wine was good, but the match was wrong. So I had some again tonight with some beef braised with juniper berries. The freshness of the wine and the depth of the beef played together well. The perfect match, I think, would be this wine with Dave Tallent's short ribs. Since I can never cook ribs like his, I can only hope they add a new Australian like this to their list. Anyway, of the 6,205 bottles I hope to have coming, there are going to be more Australians than there have been. Peace, Len Evans.

Memory and the Twenty-First Amendment

The Twenty-first Amendment (1) repeals Prohibition and (2) allows states to prohibit the transportation or importation of intoxicating liquors.[1] Justice Stevens, dissenting from a recent Supreme Court opinion somewhat limiting state bans on importation, observed that the court's decision would "seem strange indeed to the millions of Americans who condemned the use of 'demon rum.'"[2] This is a sensible thing to say about Prohibition but quite an odd thing to say about an amendment repealing Prohibition. His comment was especially powerful, however odd, in light of the implication that he had personal memory of this particular bit of legislative history. In fact, one can also remember that history as a condemnation of strong drink or as a condemnation of the corruption created by the ban itself. Which memory one privileges is not purely a historical issue.

Two contemporary questions turn in part on the question of whether the amendment's penumbra is "wet" or "dry." First, the language of section 2 of the amendment prohibits the importation into any state

1. U.S. Constitution, Amendment XXI.

2. *Granholm v. Heald*, 544 U.S. 460, 496 (Stevens, J., dissenting).

Pat Baude, upon his retirement from the Indiana University Maurer School of Law in 2008. *Courtesy of Indiana University. Taken by Tom Casalini.*

"of intoxicating liquors, in violation of the laws thereof."[3] This section contains a serious ambiguity. It might, on one hand, be read simply to empower any state to pass a law banning importation. This reading would vindicate complex state regulatory regimes whose main effect is to award monopoly profits to politically favored businesses, especially wholesalers. But it might also be read only as allowing the state to ban the importation of alcohol that was otherwise outlawed—i.e., to go dry in whole or county by county. If Justice Stevens is right that the combined force of the Eighteenth and Twenty-first Amendments demonizes rum, exiling it from the Constitution, then the first reading seems logical enough and the varying lawsuits challenging the current regimes are doomed.[4] The second contemporary question concerns the general regulation of alcohol in society. A typical narrow question is whether alcohol can be banned from places of sexual entertainment. A broader version of that question is to ask why we, as a society, have followed the supposedly discredited model of the Eighteenth Amendment in our marijuana laws, relying on a sweeping prohibition, even in the growing number of states that have themselves recognized medical uses of the drug.

The first version of this history is the story of the "Noble Experiment"—a story popular with viewers of *The Untouchables*. Liquor had corrupted the workingman, leading him to spend his wages on drink rather than family support, to spend his time in saloons away from his family and into a descending spiral of alcoholism and self-indulgence. The commercial alcohol interests fueled this process in the pursuit of profits, developing a system of saloons that particularly seduced immigrants away from efforts to join the American Way. In an age of reform, progressives seeking the same sort of benefit as those sought by wage and labor laws protected the health and welfare of workers, and the economic and social needs of their families, by protecting them from the attacks by the liquor industry. Unfortunately, organized crime and corrupt politicians conspired to profiteer on the weakness of the flesh. In the end, the wickedness of these criminals could not overcome the good of sobriety, and repeal was a necessary evil.

---

3. U.S. Constitution, Amendment XXI, § 2.
4. Patrick Baude served as the plaintiff in one such suit—*Baude v. Heath*, 538 F.3d 608 (7th Circuit 2008).

The other version of the history is a story of puritanical subversion of egalitarian democracy. The just-published work *Dry Manhattan*, by Michael Lerner, is a gripping portrayal of this point of view.[5] The Anti-Saloon League showed a mastery of single-issue pressure politics, driven substantially by nativism and hostility to Catholic and Jewish immigrants particularly. In the political system of the time, before one person one vote, over-represented rural voters imposed their religious and cultural strictures on the nation as a whole. Dissent, especially from immigrant communities, was silenced by jingoistic attacks on their patriotism. It took years for the actual will of the people to reassert itself through the convoluted amendment process. The difficulties of repeal were so extensive that Texas senator Morris Sheppard observed, "There is as much chance of repealing the Eighteenth Amendment as there is for a hummingbird to fly to the planet Mars with the Washington Monument tied to its tail."[6]

Both of these mythic versions are partially accurate descriptions of a flawed political process employed to some extent in a search for the public interest. I believe, however, that they both miss a deeper point crucial to the meaning of the constitutional experience. As the historian David Kyvig observed in 1985, "[T]he national prohibition was arguably the most radical and significant constitutional reform ever adopted."[7] Among other things, Prohibition for the first time introduced federal agents into the direct regulation of private life, essentially suspended the system of federalism and thereby altered both the public and private life of the nation.

My point here, however, is to point in a more limited way to the radical nature of the Eighteenth Amendment, in ways reinforced by both versions of the myth. The point, related to the theme of our panel about food and the law, is that food (and drink) are the essence of identity itself. Without (I hope) parodying Lévi-Strauss's *Le Cru et le Cuit*, it remains that personal

---

5. Michael Lerner, *Dry Manhattan: Prohibition in New York City* (Cambridge, MA: Harvard University Press, 2007).
6. The quote is reported many places, including Daniel Okrent, *Last Call: The Rise and Fall of Prohibition* (New York: Scribner, 2010), 330.
7. David Kyvig, *Sober Thoughts: Myths and Realities of National Prohibition After Fifty Years*, *in Law, Alcohol, and Order: Perspectives on National Prohibition* (Westport, CT: Greenwood Press, 1985), 3, 6.

identity is connected with food in ways far more intimate than any other form of consumption. Children begin to separate from their parents as they assert autonomy at the feeding table. Many nationalities are identified in slang, at least, by distinctive dietary items—“frogs,” “krauts,” “limeys” and other derogatory epithets. The place that food and wine play in Communion is only the most dramatic illustration of the centrality of this oral consumption to autonomy—indeed, one of the fascinating skirmishes of the Prohibition era was the different approach to Jewish and Catholic sacramental wine.

I suggest, in short, that a central fact of Prohibition was that it therefore regulated identity, not behavior. As such, it was an act of cultural violence to the minority rather than an ordinary law regulating behavior. A comparable contemporary act would be an English-only law that made it a crime to speak any other language—a step no nativist organization, so far as I know, has yet even proposed. The prohibition of medical marijuana, by contrast, does not regulate an incident of identity.

If I am right about the centrality of the identity-food-drink connection, the Twenty-first Amendment should then be understood as preserving to the states their right to define their own political identity rather than a general enhancement of their police powers because of the potentially harmful effects of alcohol. This would uphold partial or complete prohibition of beverage alcohol but not its economic exploitation or discriminatory regulation.

THE HERMENEUTICS OF WINE CRITICISM

Abstract: In acrimonious exchanges, contemporary critics dispute both the mechanics and the goals of wine tasting. I argue that these disputes are actually arguments familiar in literary criticism generally and should be understood in that context. This enables the reader, and the drinker, to see that the conflict is actually about values and not about wine at all.

Wine is a chemical. It has no meaning. And, as Mike Steinberger writes, "the market for wine criticism has always been a puny one."[8] Nonetheless, the contentiousness among wine writers rises almost to the level of a faculty debate over granting tenure in an English department at a contemporary American university. One reviewer, for example, derides Robert Parker's followers as believers in "faith-based wine criticism."[9] Another

8. Mike Steinberger, "Every One a Critic: The Future of Wine Writing," *The World of Fine Wine* 19 (2008): 130.
9. Tony Hendra, review of *The Emperor of Wine*, by Erin McCoy, *New York Times*, August 7, 2005.

wine writer has subtitled her book *How I Saved the World from Parkerization.*[10] This writer has herself been expunged, leaving no trace, from the widely read electronic bulletin board managed by Mark Squires, one of Parker's coauthors, and Parker in turn has referred to some of his critics as "scary wine gestapo."[11] What can bring writers to this intemperate demonstration of Godwin's Rule of Nazi Analogies? Can tempers really flare over the difference between the scent of candied black cherries and kirsch-infused raspberries?

It must be that wine critics are not writing about wine as such. My conceit is that they are arguing about the good life to which wine might be a tool rather than the wine itself. As a result, their arguments do in fact replicate the debates in other branches of critical theory. My plan in this brief contribution is to sketch out three main schools of wine writing: (1) consumerist; (2) the school of terroir; and (3) admirers of the winemaker. I then suggest that these three schools correspond to the following important movements in critical theory: (1) the new criticism; (2) critical social theory; and (3) the auteur analysis of film.

If these analogies hold, then an educated reader can bring to these texts many other intellectual experiences of aesthetic evaluation. That educated background will help him or her to sort out the ideas involved. This is worth doing because an informed discussion of wine is connected to many important questions about the good life today—connected, that is, to issues like globalization, ecology, colonialism, materialism, the concentration of wealth and bullshit.[12]

Until 1920, most writing about wine was technical and geographical. Classical texts like Columella's *De Re Rustica*, a twelve-volume agricultural treatise that devoted volume two to wine, or nineteenth-century catalogues like Charles

---

10. Alice Fiering, *The Battle for Wine and Love: Or How I Saved the World from Parkerization* (New York: Harcourt, 2008).

11. www.decanter.com/news/152889.html.

12. The first five are self-evident. For the sixth, see Harry Frankfurt, *On Bullshit* (Princeton, NJ: Princeton University Press, 2005). In connection with wine, see Richard E. Quandt, "On Wine Bullshit: Some New Software," *Journal of Wine Economics* 2 (2007): 129.

Cocks's 1843 book on Bordeaux (still in print in revised form),[13] were mainly references for the farmer or the merchant. The first book designed principally for the drinker was George Saintsbury's *Notes on a Cellar-Book* (MacMillan, 1920). Saintsbury was a literary scholar and Regius Professor at the University of Edinburgh, respected also as an amateur of wine. It is unmistakable that he wrote with the purpose of linking wine to the good life. As he said of the contents of his cellar: "When they were good they pleased my senses, cheered my spirits, improved my moral and intellectual powers, besides enabling me to confer the same benefits on other people." This appeal to self-improvement and generosity are a fairly straightforward description of the English virtues before the First World War. Saintsbury went on to make explicit that his book was a response to the temperance movement, accompanied even by a biblical text, that grapes were "fruits of that Tree of Knowledge."[14] These passages, combining sensory satisfaction, virtue and social goals, are truly the seeds for the different varieties of contemporary criticism.

The New Criticism

The "New Criticism" was a movement of the 1930s and especially after the Second World War in the United States. It emphasized reading a literary work by itself, without consulting the life or intentions of the author. The new critics intended to overthrow the paradigm of "life and works" or "life and times" that were the staple of Saintsbury's day. The name of the movement is taken from John Crowe Ransom's *The New Criticism* (1941). Key ingredients are (1) the reading of the text with precision and detail; (2) setting aside biography and cultural context; (3) ignoring the reader's response to the text (the affective fallacy); and (4) dismissing the author's intention. Supporters see these practices as "objective" and related to literary merit by

---

13. Charles Cocks, *Bordeaux and Its Wines*, ed. Bruno Boldron, 17th ed. (New York: Wiley, 2004).

14. Without the biblical references, I have tried to argue elsewhere that American Prohibition was a form of cultural violence. See "Memory and the Twenty First Amendment."

setting aside the trivial (biographical anecdotes, for example) and the cheap (readers' emotional engagement).

It is easy to translate these critical principles into a theory of wine criticism by (1) a tasting note that simply describes flavors with precision, giving specific descriptors like crème de cassis or flint, rather than descriptors like fruity or austere; (2) tasting blind, without food; (3) discounting personal preferences by evaluating all wines on the same scale, probably but not necessarily numeric; and (4) adopting the perspective of a consumer or outsider. The blind tasting without food is the essential operating method for this objective scoring process.

Compare, then, Robert Parker's own statement of the ideal critical quality of "courage." "Judgments ought to be made solely on the basis of the product in the bottle, and not the pedigree, the price, the rarity, or one's like or dislike of the producer...A judgment of wine quality must be based on what is in the bottle."[15]

LITERARY THEORY

In part a reaction to the new criticism and perhaps also to its roots in the United States, literary theory developed in the 1950s as an effort to include continental philosophy and structuralism in the act of criticizing a literary work (or anything else that might possibly have meaning). Although there are many variations or schools within the movement, these seem to be the central points: (1) literary criticism is necessarily a form of social criticism; (2) literature therefore must be critiqued within its social context; (3) the act of criticism itself must be judged rather than regarded as an independent process leading to objective truth; and (4) meaning is not inherent in the text but is a process of construction.[16]

---

15. Robert M. Parker Jr., *Parker's Wine Buyer's Guide* (New York: Simon & Schuster, 2008).

16. This is an inadequate and oversimplified summary of a contentious and subject that defies summary. Far and away the most manageable explanation is Jonathan Culler, *Literary Theory: A Very Short Introduction* (Oxford, UK: Oxford University Press, 2000).

Applied to writing about wine, the implications are something like this. (1) The experience of wine is far more than its taste and must be placed within the community that produces and drinks it; (2) "Blind tasting," the practice of writing a tasting description before knowing who made the wine where, is therefore more a game than a critique; (3) Criticism must be more than a list of flavors, colors, textures and aromas; and (4) One wine cannot be meaningfully compared with another in a way that implies comparison by anything like a numeric scale.

Among practicing wine critics, there is both a weak version and a strong version of these propositions. For the weak version, consider these statements, three of them from the eloquent and quintessentially British Hugh Johnson. (1) "Students, brokers, sommeliers, customers, children growing up in wine-growing families all form their expectations, and shape their lives, around the almost Platonic concept of what the French call the *cru.* [These]...are existential realities."[17] (2) "Blind tasting will only guarantee your 'objectivity' if that objectivity is so fragile it needs such a crude crutch. If you're too immature (or inexperienced) to be objective when necessary, tasting blind won't help you. It will, however, confuse you as to the purpose of *drinking* wine."[18] (3) "Music might be a better model for it than colours, or biology, or any of the sciences...a plethora of adjectives is all very well, but verbs are even more telling."[19] (4) "I look for the virtues proper to each wine and enjoy them for what they are."[20]

In literary theory generally, in addition to the denial of objectivity and emphasis on social construction and context, a school of thought connected with Jürgen Habermas identifies self-reflection and emancipation as the purpose of critical knowledge.[21] This "strong version" is fully reflected in the wine criticism of Jonathan Nossiter, maker of the film *Mondovino* and fervent defender of the concept of terroir: "Without this liberating notion

17. Hugh Johnson, *A Life Uncorked* (Los Angeles: University of California, 2006), 70–71.

18. Terry Theise, "Estate Selection German Catalog 2006," 21. Theise also quotes the American importer Kermit Lynch: "Blind tasting is to wine as strip poker is to love."

19. Johnson, *A Life Uncorked*, 49.

20. Ibid., 43.

21. Jürgen Habermas, *Knowledge and Human Interests* (Boston: Beacon, 1972).

of terroir—in wine, in cinema or in life...—individuality, dignity, toleration of common civilization does not exist. Terroir is an act of generosity. It is the sharing of the particular for the benefit of the whole."[22]

The Auteur

One problem with taking wine seriously is that it is not like other artistic or literary forms.[23] It is a complex agricultural product manufactured by a large team, involving many mechanical and administrative processes and driven by the economics of a substantial investment in natural resources. If we think of this process as "art" to criticize, it is hard to say who is the "artist." Is it the farmer or the winemaker or the owner who directs the winemaker and buys the grapes, as in the United States, from different growers? One analogy is to a motion picture film, which is also a complex commercial venture with many mechanical and administrative processes employing a large team but also involving the communicative arts of screenwriting, acting, music and photography.[24] The auteur theory conceives of the film as a product of the director, who deploys the players like chess pieces in pursuit of a particular vision or message. The deeper meaning of the film can then be found in the intention and collective *oeuvre* of the director. As a matter of film criticism, there are many problems with the theory. It may succeed in criticizing a film by Hitchcock or Truffaut, but it leaves out the potentially massive contributions of Anthony Hopkins or great screenwriters. Unlike the new criticism, auteur theory makes intention the key factor for the critic, and unlike literary theory, it overlooks the social community as a critical factor.

---

22. Jonathan Nossiter, *Le Goût et le Pouvoir* (Paris: Grasset 2007), 13 (my translation of the original French text).
23. See the enlightening essay by the philosopher Tim Crane, "Wine as an Aesthetic Object," in *Questions of Taste: The Philosophy of Wine*, ed. Barry C. Smith (Oxford, UK: Oxford University 2007), 141.
24. Certainly the most agreeable, and perhaps the most penetrating, resource is the guide maintained at this website of the British Film Institute: www.bfi.org.uk/filmtvinfo/publications/16+/auteur.html.

Nonetheless, the idea of affixing responsibility on one controlling figure is a way of making sense of wine. Americans, particularly, find it easy to understand the idea that Robert Mondavi or, even better, Francis Ford Coppola, the owner of Rubicon, has "directed" a wine, thereby creating something that can then be judged directly against the intent of the creator. Many wine books currently popular in the United States are, in effect, collections of biographical essays of producers like Piero Antinori,[25] Nicolas Joly,[26] Randall Grahm,[27] Hubert Lignier,[28] Georges Duboeuf[29] or female winemakers in general.[30]

THE GOOD LIFE

The parallels between literary criticism and wine writing have not escaped literary critics. Saintsbury himself, in a writing about literature, used such devices as comparing the novels of Jane Austen to "subtly flavored claret."[31] His major biographer wrote, "The methods that Saintsbury employs to criticize wine and spirits often resemble those in his literary works."[32] Of his reputation as a literary critic, she begins the biography by observing: "'King of Critics in our time…the magnificent Saintsbury.' Thus Christopher Morley hailed George Saintsbury in an introduction to *Bartlett's Quotations* in 1937. Critics of 1895 would have agreed, but not many

25. Lawrence Osborne, *The Accidental Connoisseur* (New York: North Point, 2004), 215.
26. Robert V. Camuto, *Corkscrewed* (Lincoln: University of Nebraska, 2008), 161.
27. Jay McInerney, *A Hedonist in the Cellar* (New York: Knopf, 2006), 147.
28. Neal I. Rosenthal, *Reflections of a Wine Merchant* (New York: Farrar, Straus & Giroux, 2008), 233.
29. Rudolph Chelminski, *I'll Drink to That* (New York: Gotham, 2007).
30. Ann B. Matasar, *Women of Wine* (Los Angeles: University of California, 2006).
31. George Saintsbury, *The Peace of the Augustans: A Survey of Eighteenth-Century Literature as a Place of Rest and Refreshment* (n.p.: Bell, 1916), 143.
32. Dorothy Richardson Jones, *"King of Critics": George Saintsbury 1845–1933* (Ann Arbor: University of Michigan, 1995), 278.

would have done so in Morley's time, the era of the New Criticism, because close reading of the text rather than literary appreciation and historical placing had become the chief method of criticism and teaching."[33] In any case, it seems safe to place Saintsbury's world view in the values and social practices of late Victorian England.

It seems equally clear that Robert Parker belongs to the world and values of market capitalism. Satisfaction is an economic value, not a psychic quest in the land of sentiment. The hopes and fears of winemakers, the social context of taste, the externalities imposed on conservation or public health, are real but of interest in buying wine only so long as they are internalized in the price. The duty of the wine critic is to guide the consumer through confusion and manipulation to the greatest satisfaction from the liquid itself. It does not demean Parker's personal virtue in any way to tie his view of criticism to the marketplace.

Indeed, for the consumer, the social criticism of wine critics like Hugh Johnson or Jonathan Nossiter lacks the utility of Parker's view. That, of course, is their point. They mean to liberate us from being consumers by elevating us to self-conscious members of the community. It takes a village to enjoy a glass of wine.

And perhaps finally, the auteur school of wine writing responds to the need to "understand" wine. This creative account draws on pervasive narratives of intention and skill, whose impact on the world makes it comprehensible without requiring the reader to learn any chemistry or sociology. At its worst, the biographical approach to wine, as to art, can feed celebrity culture that replaces an honest meal with a telegenic chef. But at its best, it is a celebration of individuality rather than utility or culture.

---

33. Ibid., vii.

A Tribute to Pat Baude

By Christine Barbour

It's been a cherished tradition around here for more than a decade—the night the "carry-out cheese guy" delivers. There is no carry-out cheese guy, really; he was just an invention of my friend Pat, fabricated to drive home the point that the nights we shared cheese and wine were casual, relaxed affairs requiring nothing of the host other than the mail-ordering of cheese, maybe the grilling of some vegetables and the purchasing of cookies, to be nibbled at, slowly, by people who were too stuffed to breathe but who required a mouthful of something sweet before calling it a night.

We'd started off ordering cheese from a French company that offered a wine and cheese "seminar"—packaging together fromages et vin with tasting notes that were hilarious for their eccentric translations. Eventually it was clear that Pat knew as much about wine—and a heck of a lot more about English—as the authors of the tasting notes, and we gave up the seminars for our own efforts at matchmaking. Cheese nights became regular affairs, long, effervescent evenings of food, wine, conversation and fun in the company of Pat and his wife, Julia.

We lost Pat in January, and all the fizz has gone flat.

One of the real joys of being a food person in Bloomington was palling around with Pat—a gourmand if there ever was one. Pat was always up for a food tasting—not only of wine and cheese but also pizza, vinegar, bacon, beef and odd condiments. He might sit quietly through the sips and slurps, nibbles and bites, but if you were lucky enough to lay your hands on his

Pat Baude, in 2002, giving the Fuchs lecture and being awarded the Ralph F. Fuchs Chair in Law and Public and Service. *Courtesy of Indiana University*.

tasting notes afterward, there you would find it in all its stinging, sometimes poetic judgment. An aged sherry vinegar tasted of "figs, raisins and other dark things," a mediocre pizza was "trite" and a pink Himalayan salt was, what else? "Salty."

A large man who lived larger, Pat's wit and wide knowledge dominated the table whether he chose to hold forth on it or not. With so much reason to show off, he really never did. Ever the teacher, he let you come to your judgment before sharing his, maybe, if you asked and if he was feeling expansive. But often he was a quiet observer, making mental notes. You only had to mention a favorite food or eating quirk to find it catered to on your next meal at their house. Did I like this cheese or that? I might not remember, but Pat surely did.

I don't pretend to have unraveled the complexities of Pat during the years that I knew him, and I am certain that that is how he would have preferred it. But part of the fun of Pat was being surprised by who he turned out to be. Intensely private, he yet aired bits of his life first through his blog and then his wine column. Intimidating when he cared to be, he was also shy in ways as unexpected as they were touching in such a big and capable man. Frighteningly smart, he would listen with respect (though occasionally with an arched eyebrow or a twinkle) to a fumbling student (I was one of those too, once, in Professor Baude's classroom). Distinguished and dignified, he'd willingly tolerate the launching onto his person of an unsteady old dog who knew instinctively that he would find a welcome on Pat's lap. Realistic and often bitingly cynical, he was nonetheless a romantic, holding out for the little guy, the redemption and the happy ending.

Pat was a kindred spirit, an eager palate, a dear friend and the only person I have ever known who was happy to share a long, opinionated conversation with me about vinegar.

Being a foodie in Bloomington is never going to be quite as much fun again.

A Tribute to Patrick

by His Children
(April/May 2011)

Our dad used to tell a story about a nineteenth-century Baude forebearer who was a priest in France. He lost his faith in some fashion that left him so bitter against the church, the story goes, that he bought a house next to a convent for the express purpose of roasting lamb on Friday nights with the windows open so the savory aroma of cooked meat might waft over to torment the self-denying nuns.

In retrospect, it's obvious why this story appealed to Dad, who was kicked out of Sunday school as a kid for asking too many questions. For him, too, the palate was a medium for self-expression.

Though our father was brilliantly articulate, when it came to showing his love, he often let his kitchen do the talking. Even the proverbial Italian grandmother would be utterly outdone by the extent to which he expressed his love at the dinner table. His attentiveness to the tastes of the people he cared about was extraordinary yet unobtrusive. You could almost think it was just happy chance that you liked what you found on your plate—and in your glass—better and better with every meal. And Dad would always feign a moment of surprise, as if he didn't know full well he'd just served you your new favorite thing.

In one of his *Bloom* columns, he described the dilemma of figuring out what wine to serve when his children came for dinner. One of us (William)

Pat Baude smiling over a glass.
Courtesy of Bloom Magazine.

loved so-called fruit bombs, overwhelming Californian and Australian wines that are delicious but never subtle. Another of us (Leora) preferred minerally, cerebral French wines, which skeptics would describe as tasting like dirt. Jonathan had not taken to wine at the time (a mistake Dad patiently waited out), but his tastes have ended up someplace in between—which Dad recognized long before Jonathan did. And Virginia gets headaches from everything but Champagne. Dad loved the challenge of finding ways to share what he loved with all of us.

Wine had special resonance to him as the son of a Frenchman. He has written about the last bottle of wine he shared with his father, in 1980—Chateau d'Yquem—and he saw the wine he inherited as a link between father and son. It was good to hear from a wine-loving friend to whom he had spoken of these things that he wanted to leave the same kind of gift to his kids.

A 1990 Chateau d'Yquem from Pat Baude's cellar (and now in William's).

He often bought wine with purpose—for a particular person with whom he planned to share it and even a particular occasion on which he planned to do so. Just last Christmas, he was showing us some new bottles and making plans to drink them with us in five or ten or fifteen years. Laying out bottles in the cellar was his way of laying out the future. Maybe his wine is a way for us to stay connected to him for a while yet.

Of course, there is more to life than wine. Since Dad died in January, we have been overwhelmed by just how many people remembered and admired him in so many different ways—as a cook, as a lawyer, as a teacher, as a friend. And in each of these domains, people have described the same traits—brilliance, humor, stubbornness and a deep desire to share his passions with everybody around him. They made him an extraordinary law professor, a great wine columnist and a much loved dad.

William, Jonathan, Leora and Virginia Baude

Places in Bloomington

Big Red (discussed throughout) is a large wine and liquor store with thirteen locations in Bloomington. The main one is at 418 North College Avenue.

Bloomingfoods is a cooperative, member-owned grocery store with multiple locations in Bloomington. Its original location is at 419 East Kirkwood Avenue.

Bloomington Brewing Company (Lennie's) serves pizza, salads and sandwiches, in addition to the beer (discussed in "Here's to Beer!"). It is located at 1795 East Tenth Street.

FARMBloomington is a quirky restaurant run by chef Daniel Orr, featuring local foods, as well as a small market of gifts and special prepared food items. It is located at 108 East Kirkwood Avenue.

Finch's Brasserie (mentioned in "Here's to Beer!" and "When to Send that Bottle Back") is a restaurant highlighting local and seasonal foods and also features a wood-burning oven and an extensive beer and wine list. It is located at 514 East Kirkwood Avenue and was formerly known as Trulli Flatbread.

Goods for Cooks sells a carefully selected assortment of cooking supplies and gourmet pantry items. It is located at 115 North College Avenue.

Big Red Liquors' original location.

Restaurant Tallent.

The Sahara Mart's original location.

Little Zagreb is discussed in "No Need to Show Off When Ordering Wine" and is located at 223 West Sixth Street.

Oliver Winery (mentioned in "Spring Is Time to Try a New Grape" and elsewhere) is a local winery that has made wine for forty years. It was the creation of Indiana University law professor William Oliver. It is located at 8024 North State Road 37.

Restaurant Tallent (discussed throughout) is a phenomenal restaurant, featuring local ingredients and quality wines, run by Dave and Krissy Tallent. It is located at 208 North Walnut Street.

The Sahara Mart (discussed throughout) is an eclectic grocery store, including a wide variety of international and ethnic offerings and a wide variety of wine and beers. Its original location is at 106 East Second Street. A second, larger store is now at 2611 East Third Street.

Tutto Bène was a wine bar in downtown Bloomington, but it is now closed.

The Upland Brewing Company serves assorted pub food and is especially famous for its buffalo burgers, in addition to the beer (discussed in "Here's to Beer!"). It is located at 350 West Eleventh Street.

The Uptown Cafe (discussed in "No Need to Show Off When Ordering Wine") is a long-standing local favorite with many Cajun influences. It is located at 102 East Kirkwood Avenue.

About the Author

Patrick L. Baude was born in Independence, Kansas, in 1943. He earned a JD from the University of Kansas and an LLM from Harvard. He was then a professor at the Indiana University Maurer School of Law from 1968 to 2008 and was named the Ralph F. Fuchs Professor of Law and Public Service. He continued to teach after retirement. He also wrote about wine, becoming the wine columnist for *Bloom Magazine* in 2006 and continuing to write until his death in January 2011.

Visit us at
www.historypress.net